Droid™ 4

FOR

DUMMIES®

Droid™ 4

FOR

DUMMIES®

by Dan Gookin

WILEY

John Wiley & Sons, Inc.

Droid™ 4 For Dummies®

Published by
John Wiley & Sons, Inc.
111 River Street
Hoboken, NJ 07030-5774

www.wiley.com

Copyright © 2012 by John Wiley & Sons, Inc., Hoboken, New Jersey

Published by John Wiley & Sons, Inc., Hoboken, New Jersey

Published simultaneously in Canada

For general information on our other products and services, please contact our Customer Care Department within the U.S. at 877-762-2974, outside the U.S. at 317-572-3993, or fax 317-572-4002.

For technical support, please visit www.wiley.com/techsupport.

Wiley publishes in a variety of print and electronic formats and by print-on-demand. Some material included with standard print versions of this book may not be included in e-books or in print-on-demand. If this book refers to media such as a CD or DVD that is not included in the version you purchased, you may download this material at http://booksupport.wiley.com. For more information about Wiley products, visit www.wiley.com.

Library of Congress Control Number: 2012937948

ISBN 978-1-118-33674-8 (pbk); ISBN 978-1-118-35183-3 (ebk); ISBN 978-1-118-35185-7 (ebk); ISBN 978-1-118-35186-4 (ebk)

Manufactured in the United States of America

10 9 8 7 6 5 4 3 2 1

WILEY

About the Author

Dan Gookin has been writing about technology for over 20 years. He combines his love of writing with his gizmo fascination to create books that are informative, entertaining, and not boring. Having written more than 120 titles with millions of copies in print translated into over 30 languages, Dan can attest that his method of crafting computer tomes seems to work.

Perhaps his most famous title is the original *DOS For Dummies,* published in 1991. It became the world's fastest-selling computer book, at one time moving more copies per week than the *New York Times* #1 bestseller (though as a reference, it could not be listed on the NYT Bestseller list). From that book spawned the entire line of *For Dummies* books, which remains a publishing phenomenon to this day.

Dan's most popular titles include *PCs For Dummies*, *Droid X For Dummies*, *Word For Dummies*, and *Laptops For Dummies*. He also maintains the vast and helpful website, www.wambooli.com.

Dan holds a degree in Communications/Visual Arts from the University of California, San Diego. Presently, he lives in the Pacific Northwest, where he enjoys spending time with his sons playing video games inside while they watch the gentle woods of Idaho.

Publisher's Acknowledgments

We're proud of this book; please send us your comments at http://dummies.custhelp.com. For other comments, please contact our Customer Care Department within the U.S. at 877-762-2974, outside the U.S. at 317-572-3993, or fax 317-572-4002.

Some of the people who helped bring this book to market include the following:

Acquisitions and Editorial

Project Editor: Susan Pink

Acquisitions Editor: Katie Mohr

Copy Editor: Susan Pink

Editorial Manager: Jodi Jensen

Editorial Assistant: Leslie Saxman

Sr. Editorial Assistant: Cherie Case

Cover Photo: background: © istockphoto.com/EvgenyKuklev; foreground (hand): © istockphoto.com/zentilia; image of phone and screenshot created by author

Composition Services

Project Coordinator: Katherine Crocker

Layout and Graphics: Carrie A. Cesavice, Corrie Niehaus, Erin Zeltner

Proofreader: Dwight Ramsey

Indexer:
BIM Indexing & Proofreading Services

Publishing and Editorial for Technology Dummies

Richard Swadley, Vice President and Executive Group Publisher

Andy Cummings, Vice President and Publisher

Mary Bednarek, Executive Acquisitions Director

Mary C. Corder, Editorial Director

Publishing for Consumer Dummies

KathleenNebenhaus, Vice President and Executive Publisher

Composition Services

Debbie Stailey, Director of Composition Services

Contents at a Glance

Table of Contents

Introduction

*W*hat's in a name? A Droid by any other name would still be a copyrighted trademark of the Lucasfilm Corporation. But in the context of a cell phone, it's a wonderful device that provides marvelous communications capabilities, coupled with the potential to confuse the living bajeebers out of you.

Fret not, gentle reader.

This book is designed to cover the basic operations and successful domination of the dratted curse of the 21st century: the modern cell phone. In this case, the book you hold in your hands is specific to the Motorola Droid 4 smartphone, available on the Verizon network.

At this point, you can probably stop reading this Introduction as most people do. In fact, most people never even get this far, so I congratulate you. If you choose to continue reading, you'll be informed about this book, find some useful information, and suddenly discover how powerful, popular, and good-looking you are. Promise.

About This Book

The book you hold in your hands was not meant to be read from cover to cover. Don't even try. This book is a reference, so it's designed to be used as you need it. Look up a topic in the table of contents or the index. Find something about your phone that vexes you or piques your curiosity. Look up the answer and get on with your life.

Each chapter is written as its own self-contained unit, covering a specific topic about using your Droid 4. The chapters are further divided into sections that represent a task you perform with the phone or explain how to get something done. Sample sections in this book include:

- Typing on your Droid 4
- Phoning someone you call often
- Forwarding a text message

- Talking and video chat
- Listening to live music from the Internet
- Recording a video message
- Tethering the Internet connection
- Creating a Smart Action

Every section explains a topic as though it's the first one you read in this book. Nothing is assumed, and everything is cross-referenced. Technical terms and topics, when they come up, are neatly shoved to the side, where they're easily avoided. The idea here isn't to learn anything. This book's philosophy is to help you look it up, figure it out, and get back to your life.

Still reading? Good.

How to Use This Book

This book follows a few conventions for using your Droid 4, so pay attention!

The main way to interact with the modern smartphone is by using its *touchscreen,* which is the glassy part of the phone as it's facing you. Buttons also adorn the phone, all of which are explained in Chapter 2.

You can touch the screen in various ways, as described in Chapter 2.

Chapter 3 discusses text input on the Droid 4, which involves using something called the *onscreen keyboard.* Because your Droid 4 comes with a physical keyboard, which I call the *sliding keyboard,* you'll probably use that for your typing duties more than that silly onscreen keyboard. And if the mere thought of typing disgusts you, rest assured that you can avoid typing by using the phone's handy dictation feature, also covered in Chapter 3.

This book directs you to do things on your phone by following numbered steps. Every step involves a specific activity, such as touching something on the screen; for example:

3. Choose Downloads.

This step directs you to touch the text or item on the screen labeled Downloads. You might also be told to do this:

3. Touch Downloads.

Various phone options can be turned off or on, as indicated by a gray box with a green check mark in it, as shown in the margin. By touching the box on the screen, you add or remove the green check mark. When the green check mark appears, the option is on; otherwise, it's off.

 The QR codes in this book's margins are there to help you install recommended apps. To install the app, scan the bar code using special software you install on your phone. Chapter 12 discusses how to add apps to your phone as well as how to use the bar code scanner app.

Foolish Assumptions

Even though this book is written with the gentle handholding required by anyone who is just starting out, or who is easily intimidated, I have made a few assumptions.

Number one: I assume that you're still reading the introduction. That's great. It's much better than getting a snack right now or checking to see which movie the FX channel is playing over and over again this month.

My biggest assumption: You have a Droid 4 phone. Although this book could be used with other, similar phones, this one is quite specific to the Droid 4 model. In fact, if you have another phone, I recommend getting my *Android Phones For Dummies* title instead, as it's more generic.

I also assume that you have a computer, either a desktop or laptop. The computer can be a PC, or Windows, computer or a Macintosh. Oh, I suppose it could also be a Linux computer. In any event, I refer to your computer as "your computer" throughout this book. When directions are specific to a PC or Mac, the book says so.

Programs that run on your Droid 4 are called *apps*, which is short for *applications*. A single program is an *app*.

Finally, this book assumes that you have a Google account, but if you don't, Chapter 1 explains how to configure one. Do so. Having a Google account opens up a slew of useful features, information, and programs that make using your phone more productive.

Still reading? Impressive. Here's a bonus: Stick your finger in your ear and scratch. That's the sound the old Pac Man video game made.

Icons Used in This Book

Various icons adorn this book's margins. In addition to the QR codes (discussed earlier), you'll find the following traditional *For Dummies* book icons:

This icon flags useful, helpful tips or shortcuts.

This icon marks a friendly reminder to do something.

This icon marks a friendly reminder *not* to do something.

This icon alerts you to overly nerdy information and technical discussions of the topic at hand. Reading the information is optional, though it may win you a pie slice in *Trivial Pursuit.*

Where to Go from Here

There. Now don't you feel more powerful, popular, and better-looking than you did before you read this introduction? I told you so.

Your task now: Start reading the rest of the book — but not the whole thing, and especially not in order. Peruse the table of contents and find something that interests you. Or look up your puzzle in the index. When these suggestions don't cut it, just start reading Chapter 1.

My e-mail address is dgookin@wambooli.com. Yes, that's my real address. I reply to all e-mail messages I receive; you get a quick reply if you keep your question short and specific to this book, and providing that I'm not in the throes of missing another deadline. Although I enjoy saying "Hi," I cannot answer technical support questions, resolve billing issues, or help you troubleshoot your phone. Thanks for understanding.

You can also visit my web page at www.wambooli.com for more information or as a diversion.

For technical updates to the book, go to http://www.dummies.com/go/droid4fdupdates.

Enjoy this book and your Droid 4!

Chapter 1

Your New Phone

The Droid 4 represents the latest iteration of the popular Droid line of cell phones from Motorola. It's unique in that it offers a physical keyboard, plus 4G LTE speeds when accessing the Internet. Such an amazing device requires a careful and dignified setup and configuration. All that information is found in this chapter, save for the dignified part.

An Out-of-the-Box Experience

I believe you'll find that your personal electronic devices behave best and fastest when removed from the confines of the box they came in. The same holds true for your phone, though the friendly human at the Phone Store may have already liberated and assembled your Droid 4 for you. If not, you can experience the thrill for yourself first-hand.

Whether your phone was manhandled by the Phone Store employee or not, you should look for some specific items inside the phone's compact and utilitarian package:

✔ The phone itself, which may be fully assembled or in two or more pieces

✔ The warranty, a warning, and perhaps a tiny useless *Master Your Device* pamphlet

- The phone's battery, which might already be installed inside the phone

- The phone's back cover, which also might already be on the phone

- The charger/data cable, or USB cable

- The charger head, which is a wall adapter for the charger/ data cable

- The back cover key

You may find other stuff as well, including items "tossed in" by the Phone Store, including a case, a belt clip, a car mount, head-phones, and even more pieces of paper. The variety is endless, and the Phone Store human will gladly sell you whatever your wallet can afford.

If anything is missing or appears to be damaged, immediately contact the folks who sold you the phone.

 I recommend keeping the instructions and other information as long as you own the phone: The phone's box makes an excellent storage place for that stuff — as well as for anything else you don't plan to use right away.

Setting up the Droid 4

I know of no phone that pops right out of the box ready to make phone calls. As with certain toys, some assembly is required. Here's the basic outline of what you need to do:

1. **Remove the back cover from its plastic cocoon.**

2. **Install the SIM card.**

3. **Assemble the phone.**

The cheerful employee in the Phone Store might have completed all these steps for you. If not, refer to the sections that follow for specific directions.

One task you might end up doing yourself is removing the protective plastic sheets found on the phone's screen and various other locations. Those plastic sheets protect the phone, but also tell you where important things are located. You can remove all the plastic clingy sheets at this time.

✔ You'll need to slide open the Droid 4 keyboard to remove the clingy plastic sheet from the back of the touchscreen part of the phone.

✔ One thing that the Droid 4 doesn't come with is a microSD card.

✔ The Droid 4 does not come with a removable battery. So unlike other Android phones, you do not need to install the phone's battery as part of its initial setup.

✔ After initial setup, and optionally installing the micro-SIM and microSD cards (covered in the sections that follow), my advice is to charge the phone's battery. See the later section "Charge the Battery."

Removing the phone's back cover

You remove the Droid 4's back cover for three reasons: to install or replace the micro-SIM card, to install or replace the microSD card, and to sate your infernal curiosity about what mysteries dwell inside your phone.

To remove the Droid 4's back cover, follow these steps:

1. **Insert the back cover removal tool into the hole at the top-right corner of the phone's rump.**

   Use Figure 1-1 as your guide.

   When you lose the back cover removal tool, use an unbent paper clip instead.

2. **Press gently with the removal tool, then tug the back cover downward slightly, as illustrated in Figure 1-1.**

   Don't force the removal tool into the hole! Only a gentle push is required to get the job done. (You're simply pushing down on the back cover locking tab, which allows you to slide down the back cover.)

   You can stop pressing gently with the removal tool when the back cover begins to slide freely.

3. **Pop off the back cover and set it aside.**

   You'll need to pry off the cover. A series of tabs hook into slots on the back of the phone. Each tab must be pulled from its slot, so don't think that you're breaking anything.

Removal tool you'll inevitably lose

Release hole

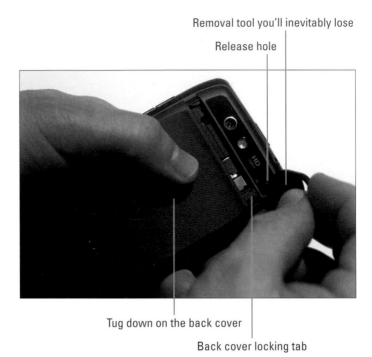

Tug down on the back cover

Back cover locking tab

Figure 1-1: Removing the back cover.

Refer to the next two sections for information on inserting or removing the micro-SIM card and microSD card.

See the section "Closing the phone" for information on replacing the back cover.

Installing the micro-SIM card

Your Droid 4 needs a micro-SIM card to uniquely identify itself with and access the 4G LTE digital cellular network. Because it's such an important part of your phone, the SIM card was most likely installed by the human at the Phone Store. If not, you can follow these steps to insert the SIM card into your phone:

1. **If necessary, remove the phone's back cover.**

   Refer to the preceding section.

2. **Remove the micro-SIM card from its container.**

3. **Insert the micro-SIM card into its slot inside your phone.**

You'll need to lift the plastic grommet below the rear camera lens to access the micro-SIM card slot. The grommet is illustrated in Figure 1-2. Lift the grommet by its left end, as shown in the figure.

The SIM card is shaped in such a way that it's impossible to insert it improperly. Use the outline inside the phone to properly orient the card and shove it into the slot.

4. **Replace the phone's back cover now — or later.**

   If you haven't installed the microSD card, don't replace the phone's back cover and do read the next section.

Micro-SIM card

Plastic grommet thing

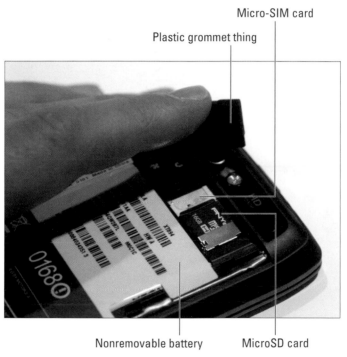

Nonremovable battery   MicroSD card

Figure 1-2: Inserting the micro-SIM card.

SIM stands for Subscriber Identity Module, just in case you play crossword puzzles. The *micro* part means that the card is smaller than the typical phone SIM card.

Installing a microSD card

I highly recommend that you get a microSD card for your Droid 4. Don't delay! Do it now!

Why are you still reading this? Get that microSD card! Sheesh . . .

After you obtain the card, install it in your Droid 4 by obeying these steps:

1. **If necessary, remove the phone's back cover.**

   The microSD is installed in the top part of the phone's exposed rear, just below the text *HD 1080p* by the camera's LED flash. (Refer to Figure 1-2 for the specific location.)

2. **Lift the rubber grommet to access the microSD slot.**

   The grommet is found just below the camera lens.

3. **Insert the microSD card into the slot.**

   The card goes in only one way; use the outline next to the slot to properly orient the card.

4. **Ensure that the card is fully inserted.**

   Push it in as far as it will go.

5. **Reassemble the phone.**

If you need to remove the card later, open up the phone, lift the grommet, and pull out the microSD card using your fingernail.

✔ Get an 8GB microSD card at minimum. The Droid 4 can handle microSD cards of 16GB and even 32GB capacities.

✔ The storage on the microSD card supplements the 16GB of internal storage that comes with your Droid 4.

✔ MicroSD cards are teensy! Keep them in a safe place where you won't lose them.

✔ You can buy an adapter for your microSD card to allow its data to be read by computers, through either a standard SD (Secure Digital) memory slot or the USB port.

✔ After you insert the microSD card and turn on the phone, you may see a microSD card notification, as shown in the margin. Pull down the notifications (directions are offered in Chapter 2) and choose the Format SD Card notification. Obey the directions on the screen to prep the microSD card.

Closing the phone

After your brief stint as a phone surgeon, you need to close the patient:

1. **Place the Droid 4's rear cover on the phone.**

   Set the back cover down so that the little back cover locking tab at the top of the cover (refer to Figure 1-1) can easily slide into its slot. At that position, the plastic tabs on the side of the cover fit easily into their slots on the phone.

2. **Slide the cover back up into position.**

   The cover locks into place.

When the back cover is on properly, you should see no gaps or raised edges. If the cover doesn't seem to go on all the way, try again. Never force it!

Charge the Battery

The phone's battery may have enough oomph in it to get you started, but not enough to safely remove the device from its box and frolic carefree in the real world. My advice: One of the first things you should do is charge the phone. Heed these steps:

1. **If necessary, assemble the charging cord.**

   Connect the charger head (the plug thing) to the USB cable that comes with the phone. They connect in only one way.

2. **Plug the charger head and cable into a wall socket.**

3. **Plug the phone into the USB cable.**

   The charger cord plugs into the micro-USB connector, found on the phone's left side. The connector plugs in only one way.

The phone may turn on when you plug it in for a charge. That's okay; keep reading in this chapter to find out what to do the first time the phone turns on. You also may need to contact your cell provider for additional setup instructions before you turn on the phone.

  ✔ I recommend fully charging the phone before you use it.

  ✔ You can use the phone while it's charging.

  ✔ The phone also charges itself when it's plugged into a computer by way of a USB cable. The computer must be on for charging to work.

  ✔ Cell phones charge more quickly when plugged into the wall as opposed to a computer's USB port or a car adapter.

Hello, Phone

Your Droid 4 will most likely be on all the time. Rare is the occasion when you will turn off your phone, but it does happen. Even rarer is the first time you turn on your phone, which requires working through initial setup. No matter how you say "Hello" to your phone, it's covered in this section.

Turning on your phone for the first time

The first time your Droid 4 was turned on was probably at the Phone Store. In fact, the cheerful Phone Store employee most likely performed the initial setup procedure for you, perhaps even assisting you with setting up your Google account as well as Facebook and other accounts. If so, great. You've already experienced the thrill of turning on your phone for the first time.

If you're on your own, the first-time setup is your responsibility. The process is not terrible: Start the phone by pressing the Power/Lock button for a second or so. (The Power/Lock button is found atop the phone, in the center.)

Watch the front of the phone, the touchscreen. After the initial phone animation, some prompts are displayed. Heed the directions: Touch the Android icon and then continue to work through the steps until setup is complete.

Here are some hints and suggestions to help you complete the setup process:

- Phone activation is what gets your new Android phone communicating with the cellular network. Once activation is completed, your phone can send and receive calls, as well as access the Internet and other digital services.

- You can use the Droid 4's physical keyboard to perform your typing duties or you can touch a text box on the screen to summon the onscreen keyboard. See Chapter 3 if you need some tips or suggestions on using the phone's keyboards.

- Text typed in a password field appears briefly but is then replaced by black dots. The dots prevent prying eyes from purloining your password.

- When prompted for location services, make sure that you activate them all. You need those services to best use the phone's mapping and location capabilities.

✔ After the initial setup, you're taken to the Home screen. Chapter 2 offers more Home screen information, which you should probably read right away, before the temptation to play with your new phone becomes unbearable.

Turning on the Droid 4

After the initial setup is complete, turning on your Droid 4 is rather uneventful: Press and hold down the Power/Lock button for a few moments. Eventually you'll see the phone's startup animation. After viewing the entertaining graphics, you are presented with the main lock screen, illustrated in Figure 1-3.

Unlock the phone by touching the padlock icon (refer to Figure 1-30) and, keeping your finger on the touchscreen, sliding your finger all the way to the right side of the screen. As you slide your finger, the lock tab moves across the screen, indicating that you're unlocking the phone.

Slide right to unlock the phone

Slide up to silence the phone

Slide left to unlock the phone and use the Camera app

Figure 1-3: Unlocking the Droid 4.

You need a Google account!

To get the most from your new phone, you need a Google account. If you have one, great. If not, you need to visit www.google.com to set up an account right now. At the main Google page, click the Sign In link, then click the link to create a new account. Continue obeying the directions on the web until your Google account is created.

By setting up your Google account, you coordinate whatever information you have on the Internet with your Droid 4. That information includes your e-mail and contacts on Gmail, appointments on the Google Calendar, and information and data from other Google Internet applications. The best news? All these Google services are free.

Upon success, the phone is unlocked and you'll see the Home screen, which is where all the action takes place. Chapter 2 discusses the many things you can do at the Home screen.

- It's not necessary to unlock the phone for an incoming call. For information on receiving phone calls, see Chapter 4.

- You can also unlock the phone by sliding the camera icon (refer to Figure 1-3) to the left. Doing so unlocks the phone and starts the Camera app, so that the phone is ready to take a picture or shoot a video. See Chapter 9 for details.

- To silence the phone, slide up the speaker icon, shown in Figure 1-3. To un-silence the phone, slide the icon down again. Also see Chapter 2 for more phone-silencing information.

- In addition to the simple lock screen (refer to Figure 1-3), your Droid 4 has several lock screens that offer more protection: a pattern lock screen, a PIN lock screen, and a password lock screen. See Chapter 15 for information on configuring those lock screens.

Unlocking the phone

Most of the time you use your Droid 4 it won't be turned off. Instead, the phone will be locked. To use the phone, you have to unlock it: Quickly press the Power/Lock button, found atop the phone. By pressing the Power/Lock button you rouse the phone from its slumber, where you'll immediately see the main lock screen (refer to Figure 1-3).

You can also unlock the phone by extending its sliding keyboard, or by connecting the phone to the USB cable.

> ✔ Unlocking the phone might also be referred to as "waking up the phone," though it's not really asleep. See the later section "Putting the Droid 4 to sleep."
>
> ✔ Also see the section "Locking the phone," later in this chapter, for information on how to lock the phone.
>
> ✔ The Droid 4 is still on when it's locked. It can receive calls, play music, fetch e-mail, and perform other automatic activities. The touchscreen, however, is off while the phone is locked.

Goodbye, Phone

Just as you can say "Hello" to you phone in several ways, you can say "Goodbye" in several ways too. Which method you choose depends on how long you plan on being away from your phone and how quickly you need to say "Hello" again. These various methods are covered in this section.

Setting up your other accounts

A Google account is pretty much mandatory for your Droid 4, but you probably have more online accounts than just Google. It's possible, and often necessary, to associate those accounts with your phone. You can complete the process when you first set up the Droid 4 or at any time by following these steps:

1. **Go to the Home screen.**

   Refer to Chapter 2 for more information on the Home screen and how to get there.

2. **Press the Menu soft button.**

3. **Touch the Settings command.**

4. **Choose Accounts.**

5. **Touch the Add Account button.**

6. **Choose an account type to add from the Set Up Accounts screen.**

   For example, touch the Facebook button to add your Facebook account.

7. **Continue following directions on the screen, typing your account name, password, and other information to set up the account.**

   Also see Chapter 6 for details on configuring your Droid 4 to send and receive non-Gmail e-mail.

Locking the phone

The most common way to dismiss the Droid 4 is to press and release the Power/Lock button. The touchscreen immediately goes dark, and the phone is locked.

While the phone is locked, it will continue to play music, receive information from the Internet (e-mail and Facebook updates, for example), and sound out alarms or other notifications. But the touchscreen is dark and the soft buttons (below the touchscreen) are disabled while the Droid 4 is locked.

- An incoming call lights up the touchscreen, displaying information about the call. See Chapter 4 for details.

- Even though an incoming call activates the touchscreen, the phone is still locked. You'll have to unlock it to access other phone features while you're on the line.

- I recommend that you lock the phone after you make or receive a call. That way, you can't accidentally touch the screen to hang up, mute, or otherwise mess with the call.

- Locking the phone also allows you to put the Droid 4 in your pocket while you're making a call — assuming, of course, that you're using headphones to talk.

- The phone automatically locks itself after you ignore it for a while. In this case, *ignoring* means that you haven't touched the screen or any other phone buttons. The regular timeout value is one minute; after one minute of ignoring your phone, it automatically locks.

- Your Droid 4 most likely will spend most of its time locked.

Putting the Droid 4 to sleep

Sometimes, locking the phone isn't enough. After all, the Droid 4 can still receive calls when it's locked. The solution is to put the phone to sleep, which works like the hibernation mode on some computers.

When the Droid 4 is asleep, it doesn't receive phone calls, talk with the Internet, or generate alarms or notifications. The phone is, essentially, turned off — but not all the way. The beauty of putting the phone to sleep is that it wakes up much faster than if you had turned the phone off all the way.

The emergency restart

Cell phones rarely get stuck, but when they do, the screen and buttons don't work. A possible solution for that situation is to restart the phone by opening the back cover, removing the battery, replacing the battery, and turning the phone back on again.

The emergency restart battery solution isn't possible on the Droid 4 because the phone lacks a removable battery. You can, however, try a workaround solution: Press and hold down the phone's Power/Lock button while simultaneously pressing the Volume Down button. Hold down both buttons for about 10 seconds to reset the phone and, with luck, fix the problem.

Here's how to put your phone to sleep:

1. **Press and hold down the Power/Lock button.**

   Eventually, you see the Phone Options menu, shown in Figure 1-4.

2. **Touch the Sleep item.**

   The phone seemingly turns itself off, but it's hibernating.

Figure 1-4: The Phone Options menu.

If you change your mind and don't want to hibernate the phone, press the Back soft button to dismiss the Phone Options menu.

The Droid 4 cannot receive phone calls while it's sleeping, but it can be turned on quickly: Press and hold down the Power/Lock button. The phone snaps back to life a lot faster than had you just turned off the phone. (See the next section.)

Turning off the phone

To turn off your Droid 4, press and hold down the Power/Lock button and choose the Power Off item from the Phone Options menu (refer to Figure 1-4). You see some animation as the phone shuts itself off. Eventually, the touchscreen goes dark.

The phone doesn't receive calls when it's turned off. Calls go instead to voice mail. See Chapter 4 for more information on voice mail.

Chapter 2

The Droid 4 Tour

*Q*uite a few classic computer games — back when they were text-only games — began with the text, "You are in a maze of twisty passages, all alike." That description serves well for any new adventure, especially when it comes to technology: The entire ordeal is like being lost in a maze where everything looks the same. What helps in both situations is a guide. For the computer game, you can summon the helpful elf-fairy. For a piece of complex electronics like your Droid 4 phone, you can use the handy orientation advice offered in this chapter.

Droid 4 Orientation

The Droid 4 feels good in your hand. It's fun to touch. But what is that doodad? What, pray tell, could that little hole be? And what is that shiny thing called?

Behold Figure 2-1. It illustrates the basic doodads found on the front and back of your Droid 4. The terms in the figure are used throughout this book and are also found in whatever scant Droid 4 documentation exists elsewhere.

Figure 2-1: Droid 4, front and back.

Not shown in Figure 2-1 is the sliding keyboard, which pops out from the left side of the phone as it's facing you. Using the sliding keyboard is covered in Chapter 3.

- ✓ The phone's Power/Lock button, which turns the phone off or on, is found atop the phone, as shown in Figure 2-1.

- ✓ The main part of the phone is the *touchscreen* display. You use the touchscreen with one or more of your fingers to control the phone, which is where it gets the name *touch*screen.

- ✓ The *soft buttons* appear below the touchscreen. They may be referred to as *feature buttons* in some documentation. See the section "Working the soft buttons" for details on how the buttons work.

- ✓ The Power/USB connector is the spot on the Droid 4 where you connect a USB cable. You use that cable to charge the phone or to communicate with a computer. See Chapter 14 for information on using the cable to connect to a computer and share files.

- ✓ The HDMI connector allows you to use the phone with an external HDMI monitor or TV set to see movies, watch slideshows, or do other interesting things. See Chapter 14.

✔ The main microphone is on the bottom of the phone. Even so, it picks up your voice loud and clear. You don't need to hold the phone at an angle for the microphone to work.

✔ The phone's volume is adjusted by using the Volume Up and Volume Down button on the phone's right side (refer to Figure 2-1).

✔ The Volume button can be used also as a zoom function when using the phone's camera. See Chapter 9 for more information.

Basic Operations and Procedures

Some devices have a definite function. For example, there is no book titled *Doorbells For Dummies* because using a doorbell is pretty obvious. Your Droid 4 phone has many useful functions, none of which may be obvious to you. Rather than sit there and be frustrated, peruse this section to orient yourself with some basic procedures for operating the Droid 4.

Working the soft buttons

Four symbols dwell on the face of the Droid 4, just below the touchscreen. These are the *soft buttons*, which perform specific functions no matter what you're doing with the phone. Table 2-1 lists the soft buttons' functions in order, from left to right.

Table 2-1		Droid 4 Soft Buttons		
Button	*Name*	*Press Once*	*Press Twice*	*Press and Hold Down*
≡	Menu	Display menu	Dismiss menu	Nothing
⌂	Home	Go to Home screen	Activate the double-tap Home launch function	Recent applications
⤺	Back	Go back, close, dismiss keyboard	Nothing	Nothing
⚲	Search	Open phone and web search	Nothing	Display Voice Actions menu

The functions listed in Table 2-1 may not work all the time. For example, when there's no menu to open, pressing the Menu soft button does nothing.

Pressing the Home soft button always takes you to the primary Home screen panel (the center one) — unless you're already viewing the main (center) panel, in which case pressing the Home soft button displays an overview of all five Home screen panels. See the later section "Discovering the Home screen panels" for details.

When you press the Home button twice, you activate the Double Tap Home Launch feature. The feature is initially configured to do nothing, but you can activate the function to run one of a handful of popular apps or perform special activities. Refer to Chapter 15 for details.

Various sections throughout this book give examples of using the soft buttons. Their icons appear in this book's margins where relevant.

Manipulating the touchscreen

The main part of the Droid 4's face is the touchscreen, which has that name because you touch it to control the phone. What you use to touch the screen is up to you: Use one finger, two fingers, or even the tip of your nose, if you like. How you touch the phone's touchscreen is described by these terms and techniques:

- ✔ **Touch:** In this simple operation, you touch the screen. Generally, you're touching an object such as a program icon, a control, or a button. You might also see the term *press* or *tap*.

- ✔ **Double-tap:** Touch the screen in the same location twice. A double-tap can zoom in on an image or a map or zoom out. Because of the double-tap's dual nature, I recommend using the pinch or spread operations instead.

- ✔ **Long-press:** Touch the screen and keep your finger down. Some operations, such as moving an icon on the Home screen, begin with the long-press. This action is also referred to as a *touch-and-hold*.

- ✔ **Drag:** Touch the screen, keep your finger down, and move your finger around. The result is that you move an object or scroll the screen contents.

- ✔ **Swipe:** A swipe is a faster version of a drag. Usually, you swipe up, down, left, or right, moving displayed material in the direction you swipe your finger. A swipe can also be called a *flick*.

✔ **Pinch:** A pinch involves two fingers, which start out separated and then are brought together. The pinch is used to zoom out on an image or a map.

✔ **Spread:** In the opposite of a pinch, you start with your fingers together and then spread them. The spread is used to zoom in.

✔ **Rotate:** Use two fingers to twist around a central point on the touchscreen, which has the effect of rotating an object on the screen. If you have trouble with this operation, pretend that you're turning the dial on a safe.

You cannot use the touchscreen while wearing gloves, unless they're specially designed for using electronic touchscreens, such as the gloves that Batman wears.

Setting the volume

The Droid 4's volume control is found on the right side of the phone as it's facing you. Press the top part of the button to raise the volume. Press the bottom part of the button to lower the volume.

A volume control works for whatever noise the phone is making when you use it: When you're on a call, the volume control sets the level of the call. When you're listening to music or watching a video, the volume control sets the media volume.

You can preset the volume of the phone, media, alarms, and notifications. See Chapter 15 for information.

"Silence your phone!"

Nothing is more annoying that having your phone play your favorite cheerful ringtone at an inopportune time. To avoid that situation, most establishments recommend that you "silence your phone." Here's how to silence your Droid 4:

1. **Wake up the phone.**

   Obviously, if the phone is turned off, you have no need to turn it on just to make it silent. So, assuming that your phone is locked, press the Power/Lock button to see the unlock screen.

2. **Slide the speaker icon up.**

   You're good.

If the phone is already unlocked, you can silence it by pressing and holding down the Power/Lock button. From the Phone Options menu, choose Silent Mode.

You can silence the phone also by pressing the Volume Down button again and again (or just holding it down) until the phone vibrates slightly. The phone is silenced.

To make the phone noisy again, simply repeat the steps in this section: Slide the speaker icon down or choose Silent Mode from the Phone Options menu.

✔ When the phone is silenced, it automatically goes into vibration mode — unless you have that feature disabled. See Chapter 15.

✔ When the phone is silenced and in vibration mode, the Vibration icon appears on the status bar.

Changing orientation

The Droid 4 features an *accelerometer* doohickey, which is used by various apps to determine in which direction the phone is pointed or whether you've reoriented the phone from an upright to a horizontal position.

Figure 2-2 illustrates vertical and horizontal orientations using the Browser app, which is the Droid 4's program for surfing the web.

Figure 2-2: Vertical orientation (left) and horizontal orientation (right).

The Browser app reorients its image no matter which way you turn the phone. Many other apps also reorient themselves, but a handful of apps don't change orientation.

    ✔ See Chapter 8 for information on using your phone to browse the web.

    ✔ The Home screen reorients itself to a horizontal presentation, but only when you extend the sliding keyboard.

     ✔ A fun app for demonstrating the phone's accelerometer is the *Labyrinth* game. You can purchase it at the Play Store or download a free version, *Labyrinth Lite*. See Chapter 12 for more information on the Play Store.

The Home Screen

Your main base of operations when you use your Droid 4 is a place called the *Home screen*. It's the first thing you see after unlocking your phone, and it's the place you go to whenever you quit an app. The Home screen is also summoned instantly whenever you press the Home soft button. Obviously, recognizing the Home screen and understanding how it works are central to getting the most from your new phone.

Looking at the Home screen

The Droid 4 Home screen is shown in Figure 2-3. When the keyboard is extended, the horizontal Home screen is displayed, as illustrated in the figure. Both orientations of the Home screen show the same number of icons and widgets, though the horizontal orientation rearranges things.

Here are some points of interest and things to identify on the Home screen:

    ✔ **Status bar:** The top of the Home screen has a thin, informative strip that I call the *status bar*. It contains notification icons and phone status icons, plus the current time.

    ✔ **Notifications:** The notification icons come and go, depending on what happens in your digital life. For example, a notification icon appears whenever you receive a new e-mail message or have a pending appointment. The section "Reviewing notifications," later in this chapter, describes how to deal with notifications.

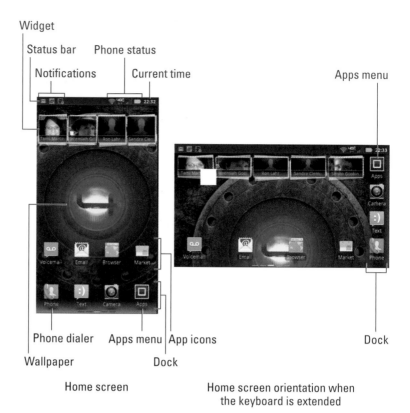

Widget

Status bar   Phone status

Notifications   Current time   Apps menu

Phone dialer   Apps menu | App icons   Dock

Wallpaper   Dock

Home screen   Home screen orientation when
                     the keyboard is extended

Figure 2-3: The Home screen.

✒ **Phone status:** Icons on the right end of the status bar represent the phone's current condition, such as the type of digital
cellular network it's connected to, the signal strength, and the
battery status, as well as whether the speaker has been muted
or a Wi-Fi network connected, for example.

✒ **Widget:** These teensy programs display information, let you
control the phone, manipulate a phone feature, access a program, or do something purely amusing. You can read more
about widgets in Chapter 15.

✒ **App icons:** The meat of the meal on the Home screen plate
are the app icons. Touching an icon runs its program, or *app.*

✒ **Dock:** The four app icons that appear on the bottom of the
screen — Phone, Text, Camera, and Apps — represent the
dock. These icons stay the same no matter which Home
screen panel you're viewing.

✒ **Phone dialer:** The official name of this app is the Phone app.
You use this app to make phone calls, peruse contacts, and
do other phone-like things.

✔ **Apps menu:** Touching the Apps icon displays the App menu, a paged list of all apps installed on your phone. The section "The App Menu," later in this chapter, describes how it works. The Apps icon always appears on the dock, in the same position: far right for the standard Home screen, or on top for the Home screen with the keyboard extended.

✔ **Wallpaper:** Behind the icons, widgets, and other detritus on the Home screen lies the *wallpaper*. It's basically the background image on your phone. See Chapter 15 for information on changing the wallpaper.

The good news: The Home screen is entirely customizable. You can add and remove icons from the Home screen, add widgets and shortcuts, and even change the wallpaper images. Chapter 15 covers the details.

Discovering the Home screen panels

The Home screen is really a whole subdivision of Home screens. Each piece of the Home screen is called a *panel*. The Droid 4 features five Home screen panels, two to the left and two to the right of the main, center Home screen panel, as shown in Figure 2-4.

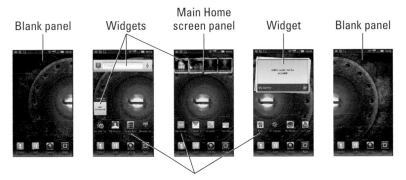

Figure 2-4: Home screen panels.

To switch between the panels, swipe your finger left or right when viewing the Home screen. As you do, another Home screen panel slides into view.

 You can see an overview of all five Home screen panels by pressing the Home soft button while viewing the center Home screen panel.

Reviewing notifications

Notifications are represented by icons at the top left of the Home screen (refer to Figure 2-1). To see what the notifications represent, peel down the top part of the screen, shown in Figure 2-5.

Notification icons   Touch here

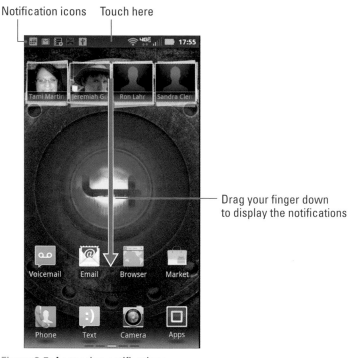

Drag your finger down
to display the notifications

Figure 2-5: Accessing notifications.

The operation works like this:

1. **Touch the status bar at the top of the touchscreen.**

2. **Drag your finger all the way down the front of the touch-screen.**

   This action works like you're controlling a roll-down blind: Grab the top part of the touchscreen and drag it downward all the way. The notifications appear in a list, as shown in Figure 2-6.

   Drag the notification list all the way to the bottom of the touchscreen to prevent it from rolling up again. Use the Notification Panel control (labeled in Figure 2-6) to pull the list all the way down.

3. Touch a notification to see what's up.

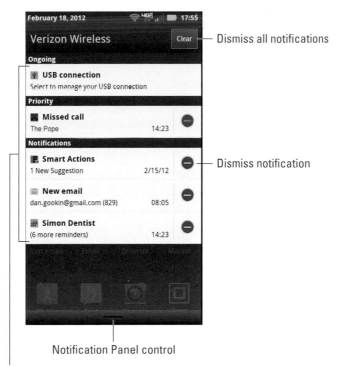

Dismiss all notifications

Dismiss notification

Notification Panel control

Touch a notification to see more information or deal with an issue

Figure 2-6: The notification list.

Touching a notification opens the app that generated the alert. For example, touching the Gmail notification displays your Gmail inbox or a specific message (if there's only one new message).

 If you choose not to touch a notification, you can "roll up" the notification list by sliding the Notification Panel control back to the top of the touchscreen or by pressing the Back soft button.

✔ A notification icon doesn't disappear until you choose it or delete it.

✔ To dismiss all notification icons, touch the Clear button (labeled in Figure 2-6).

 ✔ When more notifications are present than can be shown on the status bar, the More Notifications icon is displayed, as shown in the margin. The number on the icon indicates how many additional notifications are available.

✔ Dismissing notifications doesn't prevent them from appearing again later. For example, notifications to update installed apps continue to appear, as do calendar reminders, until those notifications are specifically dealt with.

✔ Some apps, such as Facebook and Skype, don't display notifications unless you're logged in.

✔ When new notifications are available, the notification light on the front of the Droid 4 flashes.

✔ Notification icons appear on the screen when the Droid 4 is locked. You must unlock the phone before you can drag down the status bar to display notifications.

Running an app

It's cinchy to run an app on the Home screen: Touch its icon. The app starts.

✔ Not all apps appear on the Home screen, but all of them appear when you display the App menu. See the section "The App Menu," later in this chapter.

✔ When an app closes or you quit that app, you return to the Home screen.

✔ App is short for *application*.

Working a widget

A *widget* is a teensy program that floats over the Home screen, as shown in Figure 2-3. To use a widget, simply touch it. What happens after that depends on the widget.

For example, touching the Google Search widget displays the onscreen keyboard (if the sliding keyboard isn't extended) so you can type, or dictate, something to search for on the Internet. A weather widget might display information about the current weather, social networking widgets display status updates or tweets, and so on.

Information on these and other widgets appears elsewhere in this book. See Chapter 15 for information on working with widgets.

The App Menu

The place where you find all the apps installed on your Android phone is aptly called the *App menu*. You access the App menu by touching the Apps soft button, found at the bottom right (or upper right) of the Home screen, as shown in Figure 2-3. Even though you can find and start apps from the Home screen, the App menu is the place to go when you need to find *everything*.

Viewing all the apps

Any app installed on your phone can be started from the App menu screen. Here's how it works:

1. **Touch the Apps icon on the Home screen.**

   The App menu appears, as shown in Figure 2-7. The app icons are listed alphabetically, which means A to Z for the English alphabet. For other alphabets, check a kindergarten near you.

Group menu   Google Play Store

Applications   App menu page indicator

Figure 2-7: Apps on the App menu.

2. **Ensure that All Apps is chosen from the Group menu, as shown in Figure 2-7.**

   If All Apps isn't chosen, touch the Group menu and choose All Apps.

3. **Page through the list of apps by swiping the touchscreen left or right.**

   Perusing the pages of the App menu works like flipping the pages in a book.

4. **Touch an icon to start that app.**

The app you chose opens, taking over the screen and doing whatever marvelous thing the app is supposed to do.

✒ To help you locate a lost app, or one whose name you might have forgotten, press the Search soft button while viewing the App menu. Type all or part of the app's name. As you type, items whose names match the letters you've typed appear in the list. The word *Application* appears below the program name of any application in the list.

✒ Use the Group menu to view different groups of apps, from All Apps to recently opened apps to downloaded apps to groups you create yourself.

✒ Creating app groups is covered in Chapter 12, along with information on downloading apps from the Play Store.

✒ The Apps menu contains an app named Apps. That icon lets you obtain apps from Verizon, if you want to.

✒ The terms *program*, *application,* and *app* all mean the same thing.

Reviewing recent apps

If you're like me, you probably use the same apps over and over, on both your computer and your phone. You can easily access the list of recent programs on your Droid 4 by pressing and holding down the Home soft button. When you do, you see a list of the most recently accessed programs, similar to what's shown in Figure 2-8.

Choose a recent app from the list to open that app again or to return to the app if it's already open and running.

To exit the list of recently used apps, press the Back soft button.

Group menu   Google Play Store

Recently opened applications

Figure 2-8: Apps you've opened recently.

You can press and hold down the Home soft button in any application at any time to see the recently used apps list.

For programs you use all the time, consider creating shortcuts on the Home screen. Chapter 15 describes how to create shortcuts to apps, as well as shortcuts to people and shortcuts to instant messaging and all sorts of fun stuff.

Chapter 3

Text and Typing

*I*t's difficult to believe, but typing and editing text on your Droid 4 is entirely possible. Yes, the phone is tiny, but the kind of typing that you'll do is not full-size keyboard typing but thumb typing. Along with all that typing comes text editing. Then, when your thumbs wear out from all the typing and editing, you can use the Droid 4's dictation feature and simply yell at your phone to input text. All that fun is covered in this chapter.

Keyboard Mania

As you'll discover, you can fulfill your typing desires on the Droid 4 in several ways. Most obvious is the phone's physical keyboard, what I call the *sliding keyboard*. In addition, two keyboards appear on the touchscreen: The *multitouch* keyboard and the *Swype* keyboard. All these keyboard variations are covered in this section.

✔ The three keyboards use the standard QWERTY key layout, the same as a computer keyboard. QWERTY refers to the first six letters in the top row on the keyboard.

✔ The Droid 4 sliding keyboard started out full size. But then the scientists at Motorola zapped it using that huge shrinking machine the U.S. government built under the Utah desert — you know, the same machine that shrunk Stephen Boyd and Raquel Welch in the film *Fantastic Voyage*.

Sliding out the sliding keyboard

The Droid 4 sliding keyboard is ensconced behind the touch-screen. You can slide out this keyboard (to the left as you face the phone) and use it if you prefer a physical keyboard for your cell phone typing chores.

Figure 3-1 illustrates the sliding keyboard, to call out its various parts.

Two sets of symbols share space on the sliding keyboard: one colored white and the other colored gold. The gold characters are accessed by using the Shift key; see the later section "Typing on your Droid 4" for more information about typing on the sliding keyboard.

The sliding keyboard also features direction keys: up, down, right, and left, plus the OK key. Using these keys is covered later in this chapter, in the section "Text Editing."

When you're done using the sliding keyboard, slide it back into the phone. When you do, the touchscreen may reorient itself to vertical mode or the app may stay in its horizontal orientation.

Sliding the keyboard back into the phone doesn't turn off, lock, or sleep the Droid 4.

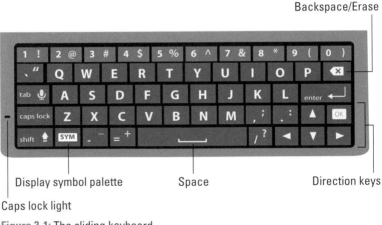

Backspace/Erase

Display symbol palette   Space   Direction keys

Caps lock light

Figure 3-1: The sliding keyboard.

Typing on the multitouch keyboard

The multitouch keyboard shows up anytime the phone demands text as input, such as when you're composing e-mail, typing a text message, or entering nuclear missile launch codes.

The alphabetic version of the multitouch keyboard is shown in Figure 3-2. The keys A through Z (lowercase) are there, plus a Shift/Caps Lock key, Delete key, space key, and period key.

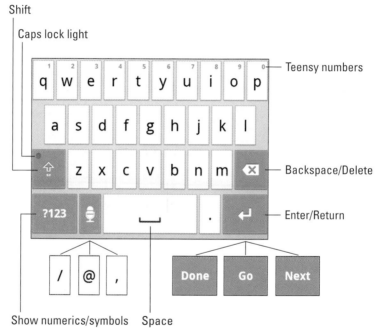

Figure 3-2: The multitouch keyboard.

The key in the lower-right corner changes its look depending on what you're typing and where you're typing it. The key has several variations, as shown in the figure. Here's what each one does:

- **Enter/Return:** Just like the Enter or Return key on a computer keyboard, touching this key ends a paragraph of text. You'll use this key mostly when filling in long stretches of text or when multiline input is available.

- **Done:** Use this key to dismiss the onscreen keyboard and view the full-screen app. Normally, this key appears whenever you finish typing text in the final field of a screen with several fields.

✔ **Go:** This action key directs the app to proceed with a search, accept input, or perform another action.

✔ **Next:** Touching the key switches from one field to the next, such as when typing a username and password. This key appears when typing information into multiple fields.

The key to the left of the space key changes as well. It can be a slash, the @ symbol, or a comma, depending on the app. In situations where voice input is accepted, the microphone icon appears. Touching the microphone icon key activates voice input, as covered later in this chapter.

?123 Touch the ?123 key to see the number keys as well as the various punctuation symbols shown in Figure 3-3, left. Pressing the Alt key on the number-and-symbol keyboard displays special symbols, also shown in Figure 3-3, right. When the Alt key has been pressed, its light turns on (as labeled in the figure).

Show alpha keyboard

Show alternative keyboard   Alternative keyboard light

1	2	3	4	5	6	7	8	9	0
@	#	$	%	&	*	-	+	(	)
ALT	!	"	'	:	;	/	?	⌫
ABC	,	␣	.	↵

~	`			•	√	π	÷	×	{	}
→		£	¢	€	°	^	_	=	[	]
ALT	™	®	©	¶	\	<	>	⌫
ABC	"	␣	...	↵

Symbol keyboard   Alt keyboard

Figure 3-3: The Symbol and Alt onscreen keyboards.

To return to the QWERTY onscreen keyboard layout (refer to Figure 3-2), touch the ABC key.

✔ Some applications show the keyboard when the phone is in landscape orientation. If so, the keyboard displays the same keys but offers more room for your stump-like fingers to type.

✔ The teensy number keys atop the QWERTY keyboard (refer to Figure 3-2) are accessed by pressing and holding down a key. For example, press and hold down the q key to type the number 1.

Using the Swype keyboard

The second variation of the onscreen keyboard is the Swype typing utility, which is designed to drastically improve your touchscreen typing speed. The secret to Swype is that you can type without lifting your finger; you literally swipe your finger over the touchscreen to rapidly type words.

Activate Swype by long-pressing any text box or location where you can type on the touchscreen. From the Edit Text menu, choose the Input Method item and then Swype. The Swype keyboard appears on the screen, replacing the multitouch keyboard.

 I understand that you probably obtained a Droid 4 to use its sliding keyboard. That's fine. But if you want to take a stab at Swype, activate the keyboard as just described and then long-press the Swype key (shown in the margin) to see the Swype Help menu. You can review the techniques for typing types of words, such as those with capital letters or double letters, and other tips. You can also touch the Tutorial button to learn how Swype works and pick up some typing tricks.

Droid 4 Hunt-and-Peck

Just when you thought you'd mastered typing on a computer, along comes typing on a cell phone. At least the Droid 4 has keyboard options. A few years back, typing on a cell phone always meant using a ten-key dialpad to input text. Things today may still be confusing, but they're far better than the hell of typing on a dialpad.

Typing on your Droid 4

Using the Droid 4 keyboards works just as you expect: Touch the key you want and its character appears in whatever app you're using. It's magic!

However, typing can be quirky, depending on which keyboard you use, as covered in the sections that follow. For both the sliding and multitouch keyboards, here are some helpful suggestions and thoughts:

- A blinking cursor on the touchscreen shows where new text appears, which is similar to how typing works on a computer.

- When you make a mistake, touch the Del key to back up and erase.

- ✔ See the later section "Text Editing" for more details on editing your text.

- ✔ Above all, *type slowly* until you get used to the keyboard.

- ✔ Misspellings and typos appear with a dashed red underline on the screen. You can long-press a misspelled word to see a list of suggestions at the bottom of the screen.

- ✔ People generally accept that composing text on a phone isn't perfect. Don't sweat it if you make a few mistakes as you type text or e-mail messages, though you should expect some curious replies from unintended typos.

- ✔ When you tire of typing, you can always touch the microphone key on the keyboard (Shift+Tab) to enter dictation mode. See the section "The Joy of Dictation," later in this chapter.

Sliding keyboard typing

Despite the capital letters on the sliding keyboard, the text you type appears in lowercase. To create a capital letter, you must press the Shift key (refer to Figure 3-1). Unlike using a computer keyboard, you don't need to hold down the Shift key; just press and release and then type a letter.

 After the Shift key has been pressed, the cursor changes its appearance, as shown in the margin. The cursor shape is your clue to the state of the Shift key.

 The cursor also changes its appearance, as shown in the margin, when the Caps Lock key has been pressed and the keyboard is in caps lock mode.

The cursor may not change its appearance in every program you use. For example, in the Browser you may see only a vertical line for the cursor.

Multitouch keyboard typing

As you type on the multitouch keyboard, each character you touch appears highlighted on the screen, as shown in Figure 3-4. In that way, you can confirm that your fingers are typing what you intended.

- ✔ To set the caps lock mode, press the Shift key twice. The little light labeled in Figure 3-2 comes on, indicating that caps lock is on.

- ✔ Press the Shift key again to turn off caps lock.

> ✔ See the later section "Choosing a word as you type" to find
> out how to deal with automatic typo and spelling corrections.

Figure 3-4: Pressing the *o* key.

Accessing special characters

You can type more characters on your phone than are shown on
either the sliding or multitouch keyboards. So don't think you're
getting gypped when you don't see the key you want.

Sliding keyboard special characters

To access special characters on the sliding keyboard, you press
the SYM key (refer to Figure 3-1). What you see is a pop-up palette
of symbols that, yes, you have to choose by touching them on the
Droid 4 screen. Figure 3-5 shows the available symbols.

Despair not if you don't see the symbol or character you're looking
for. Many more characters are available, but you have to know the
press-and-hold trick on the sliding keyboard to see them.

Figure 3-5: The SYM symbols on the sliding keyboard.

To work the press-and-hold trick, press and hold down the letter key that most resembles the symbol you want to type. For example, to type the ñ character, press and hold down the N key. A palette of accented characters appears on the touchscreen, as shown in Figure 3-6, from which you can pluck the ñ.

Figure 3-6: Accented characters for the N key.

To produce a capital accented character, press the Shift key before you press and hold down its letter key.

Touch the X button to dismiss the pop-up palette when none of the choices pleases you.

Multitouch keyboard special characters

On the multitouch keyboard, you access special characters by long-pressing a specific key. When you do, a pop-up palette of options appears, from which you choose a special character, similar to what's shown for the sliding keyboard in Figure 3-6.

The trick is to long-press a key that kind of looks like the character you want. So, for example, to produce the letter à, you press and hold down the A key and then pluck the à character from the pop-up palette.

Choosing a word as you type

As a smart phone, the Droid 4 makes a guess at the words you're typing as you type them. A list of suggestions appears above the multitouch keyboard, or at the bottom of the touchscreen when you're using the sliding keyboard. Choose a suggestion by touching it with your finger. Or, if your choice is highlighted, you can press the space key. The word you choose instantly appears on the screen, saving you time (and potentially fixing your terrible spelling or typing or both).

Text Editing

As long as you can contain your laughter, you can accept that text editing is quite possible and often necessary on your Droid 4. Although editing on the Droid 4 isn't like editing text in a word processor, a smattering of tools are available to fix random typos and otherwise rework your text, as described in this section.

Moving the cursor

The first part of editing text is to move the *cursor,* that blinking vertical line where text appears. You can move the cursor in two ways.

The easiest way to move the cursor is simply to touch the part of the text where you want the cursor to blink. This method works but is usually ineffective because your finger is probably fatter than the spot where you want the cursor.

 To help you deal with fat fingers, you can use the trapezoid icon that appears below the cursor (and is shown in the margin). Use your finger to drag the trapezoid around and position the cursor.

A second, and better, way to move the cursor is to use the direction keys, found on the sliding keyboard (refer to Figure 3-1). Pressing a direction key moves the cursor around the text in the direction of the arrow, like jabbing the arrow keys on a computer keyboard.

After you move the cursor, you can continue to type, use the Del key to back up and erase, or paste in text copied from elsewhere. See the later section "Cutting, copying, and pasting text" for more information.

Selecting text

Before text can be deleted, replaced, copied, or cut, it must be selected. This step is the traditional first step to all electronic text editing, and you're probably well-versed with the frustrations of selecting text on a computer. Well, that operation is easy compared with the convoluted and messy ways the Droid 4 has you select text, as covered in this section.

Text selection with your finger on the touchscreen

To quickly select a word, tap your finger twice on the touchscreen. The word becomes highlighted, as shown in Figure 3-7.

Pay heed to the start block and end block markers on either side of the selected word (labeled in Figure 3-7). Use your finger to drag the start and end markers around the screen, which extends the text selection.

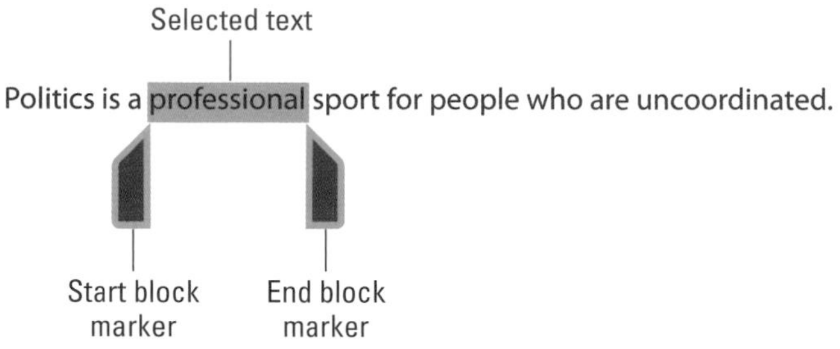

Selected text

Politics is a **professional** sport for people who are uncoordinated.

Start block marker   End block marker

Figure 3-7: Selecting a word.

As long as a single word is selected, the Droid 4 displays a list of alternatives and suggestions at the bottom of the touchscreen. To instantly replace the highlighted word, choose a new word from that list.

You can cancel the selection of text by pressing the Back soft button.

Text selection with the sliding keyboard

You can easily select tiny tidbits of text by using the sliding keyboard. Follow these steps:

1. **Extend the sliding keyboard.**

2. **Move the cursor to the location where you want to start selecting text.**

   You can use your finger, and then use the direction keys to make fine adjustments.

3. **Press and hold down the Shift key.**

4. **Use the direction keys to extend the selection up, down, left, or right.**

   The selected text appears highlighted on the screen.

At this point, you can delete or replace the text, but you can't cut or copy the text. To do that, you have to employ one of the other text selection techniques.

Text selection using the Edit Text menu

Start selecting text by pressing and holding down — a *long-press* — any part of the text screen or input box. When you do, the Edit Text menu appears, as shown in Figure 3-8.

Figure 3-8: The Edit Text selection menu.

The first two options on the Edit Text menu deal with selecting text:

- ✔ **Select Word:** Choose this option to select the word you long-pressed on the screen. You can then extend the selection as shown earlier, in Figure 3-7.

- ✔ **Select All:** Choose this option to select all text, whether it's in the input box or you've been entering or editing the text in the current application.

 To back out of the Edit Text menu, press the Back soft button.

Text selection on a web page

When you're browsing the web on your Droid 4, you select text by summoning a special menu item. Obey these steps:

1. **Press the Menu soft button to summon the web browser's menu.**

2. **Choose the More command, and then choose Select Text.**

3. **Drag your finger over the text on the web page you want to copy.**

   You can extend the selection by dragging the controls at the start or end of the text, similar to the selection shown earlier, in Figure 3-7.

4. **Touch the screen and choose the Copy command.**

   The text is instantly copied.

You can paste the text into any application on your phone that accepts text input. See the next section.

Refer to Chapter 8 for more information on surfing the web with your phone.

Cutting, copying, and pasting text

After selecting a chunk of text — or all text — on the screen, you can then cut or copy that text and paste it elsewhere. The concept of copying or cutting and then pasting text works just like it does on your computer. The steps you must follow to copy and cut text on your phone work like this:

1. **Select the text you want to cut or copy.**

   Selecting text is covered earlier in this chapter.

2. **Touch the selected text.**

   You see the Edit Text menu with these items: Cut, Copy, and Paste. (Paste appears only when you've previously cut or copied text.)

   If you don't see the Edit Text menu, try again but long-press the selected text.

3. **Choose Cut or Copy from the menu.**

   When you choose Cut, the text is removed; the cut-and-paste operation moves text. When you choose Copy, the text is copied; the copy-and-paste operation duplicates text.

4. **If necessary, start the application into which you want to paste text.**

5. **Touch the text box or text area where you want to paste the cut or copied text.**

6. **Move the cursor to the exact spot where the text will be pasted.**

7. **Long-press the text box or area.**

8. **Choose the Paste command from the Edit Text menu.**

   The text you cut or copied appears in the spot where the cursor was blinking.

The text you paste can be pasted again and again. Until you cut or copy additional text, you can use the Paste command to your heart's content.

You can paste text only into locations where text is allowed. Odds are good that if you can type text somewhere, or whenever you see the onscreen keyboard, you can paste text.

The Joy of Dictation

One of the most amazing aspects of the Droid 4 is its uncanny capability to interpret your utterances as text. It pays almost as much attention to what you say as your spouse does, though for legal reasons I can't explain why that's relevant. Suffice it to say that dictation is a boon to any cell phone user.

Dictating to your phone

 Voice input is available whenever you see the microphone icon, similar to the one shown in the margin. To begin voice input, touch the icon. The voice input screen appears, as shown in Figure 3-9.

Figure 3-9: The voice input thing.

When you see the text *Speak Now,* speak directly at the phone.

As you speak, the microphone icon (refer to Figure 3-9) flashes. The flashing doesn't mean that the phone is embarrassed by what you're saying. No, the flashing merely indicates that the phone is listening, detecting the volume of your voice.

After you stop talking, the phone digests what you said. Eventually, the text you spoke — or a close approximation of it — appears on the screen. It's magical, and sometimes comical.

- ✓ The first time you try to use voice input, you might see a description displayed. Touch the OK button to continue.

- ✓ The dictation feature works only when voice input is allowed. Not every application features voice input as an option.

- The better your diction, the better the results. Try to speak only a sentence or less.

- You can edit your voice input just as you edit any text. See the section "Text Editing," earlier in this chapter.

- You have to "speak" punctuation to include it in your text. For example, you say, "I'm sorry comma Belinda period" to have the phone produce the text *I'm sorry, Belinda*.

- Common punctuation marks that you can dictate include the comma, period, exclamation point, question mark, and colon.

- Pause your speech before and after speaking punctuation.

- There is no way to capitalize text while dictating.

- Voice Input may not function when no cellular data or Wi-Fi connection is available.

Controlling the Droid 4 with your voice

The Voice Commands app, found on the App menu, allows you to bellow verbal orders to your Droid 4. Start the app and wait a second to see a list of command suggestions.

Try out a few of the commands, such as the Call command. The phone may ask for more detailed information, requiring you to reply "yes" or "no," similar to an annoying voice menu at some Big Impersonal Company.

To cancel a voice command, say "Cancel."

Uttering f**** words

The Droid 4 features a voice censor. It replaces those naughty words you might utter, placing the word's first letter on the screen, followed by the appropriate number of asterisks.

For example, if *fudge* were a blue word and you utter *fudge* when dictating text, the Droid 4 dictation feature would place f**** on the screen rather than the word *fudge*.

The phone knows a lot of blue terms, including the infamous "Seven Words You Can Never Say on Television," but apparently the terms *crap* and *damn* are fine. Don't ask me how much time I spent researching this topic.

Chapter 4

Phone Duties

*D*espite all its fancy features and cutting-edge technology, your Droid 4, at its core, is a phone. It performs all the basic phone duties, such as making and receiving calls. It also does things that Alexander Graham Bell could barely imagine, such as call forwarding, handling multiple calls, and the weird world of voice mail. All those basic phone duties will be easier to complete after you peruse this chapter.

Make the Call

There's just no way to make it fun or fancy: The most basic use of any cell phone is making a phone call. The call is the same type of phone call people have been making for years, though the concept of "dialing" a number on a touchscreen may be new to you. Also, because the Droid 4 keeps its own address book, you can pull some time-saving tricks when dialing a phone number.

Dialing a number

To place a call on your Droid 4, heed these steps:

1. Touch the Phone app at the bottom of the Home screen.

You'll see the Phone app's Dialer screen, as shown in Figure 4-1.

Phone number

Show all matches

Dialer tab   Signal strength

Previous call/contact matches

Delete

Dialpad

Connect   Voice dial

Add number to address book

Figure 4-1: Dialing a phone number.

2. Type the number to call.

Use the keys on the dialpad to type the number. If you make a mistake, touch the Delete button (labeled in Figure 4-1), to back up and erase.

As you touch the numbers, you may hear the traditional touch-tone sound and the phone may vibrate.

Any matching contacts from the Droid 4's address book are displayed as you type the number. You can choose one of those contacts to complete the number for faster dialing.

3. Touch the green phone button to make the call.

The phone doesn't make the call until you touch the green button.

As the phone attempts to make the connection, two things happen:

- First, a Call in Progress notification icon appears on the status bar. The icon is a big clue that the phone is making a call or is actively connected.
- Second, the screen changes to show the number you dialed (see Figure 4-2). When the recipient is in the phone's address book, the contact's name, photo, and social networking status (if available) may also appear, as shown in the figure.

Even though the touchscreen is pretty, at this point you need to listen to the phone: Put it up to your ear or listen using the earphones or a Bluetooth headset.

4. **When the person answers the phone, talk.**

What you say is up to you, though it's good not to just blurt out unexpected news like "You remember that big tree in your backyard that was leaning too close to the neighbor's house?"

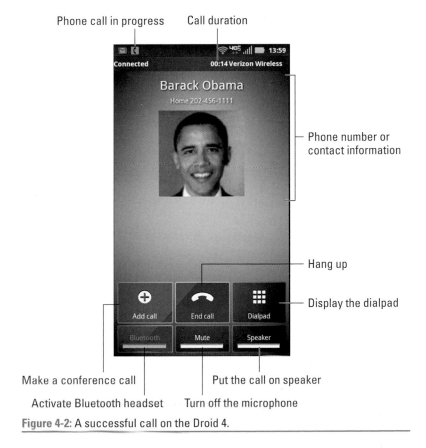

Figure 4-2: A successful call on the Droid 4.

Use the Droid 4's Volume button (on the side of the device) to adjust the speaker volume during the call.

5. **To end the call, touch the red End Call button.**

The phone disconnects. You hear a soft *beep*, which is the phone's signal that the call has ended. The Call in Progress notification goes away.

 You can do other things while you're making a call: Just press the Home button to run an application, read old e-mail, check an appointment, or do whatever. Activities such as these don't disconnect you, though your cellular carrier may not allow you to do other things with the phone while you're on a call.

To return to a call after doing something else, swipe down the notifications at the top of the screen and touch the notification for the current call. You return to the Connected screen, similar to the one shown in Figure 4-2. Continue yapping. (See Chapter 2 for information on reviewing notifications.)

- ✔ If you're using earphones, you can press the phone's Power Lock button during the call to turn off the display and lock the phone. I recommend turning off the display so that you don't accidentally touch the Mute or End button during the call.

- ✔ You can't accidentally mute or end a call when the phone is placed against your face; a sensor in the phone detects when it's close to something and the touchscreen is automatically disabled.

- ✔ Don't worry about the phone being too far away from your mouth; it picks up your voice just fine.

 - ✔ To mute a call, touch the Mute button, shown in Figure 4-2. A Mute icon, similar to the one shown in the margin, appears as the phone's status (atop the touchscreen).

- ✔ If you're using an earbud-style headset for the call, you can use the button on the headset to mute the call.

 - ✔ Touch the Speaker button to be able to hold the phone at a distance to listen and talk, which allows you to let others listen and share in the conversation. The Speaker icon appears as the phone's status when the speaker is active.

 - ✔ Don't hold the phone to your ear when the speaker is active.

- ✔ If you're wading through one of those nasty voice mail systems, touch the Dialpad button, shown in Figure 4-2, so that you can "Press 1 for English" when necessary.

✔ When using a Bluetooth headset, connect the headset *before* you make the call.

✔ You hear an audio alert whenever the call is dropped or the other party hangs up. The disconnection can be confirmed by looking at the phone, which shows that the call has ended.

✔ You cannot place a phone call when the phone has no service; check the signal strength indicator (labeled in Figure 4-1).

✔ You cannot place a phone call when the phone is in airplane mode. See Chapter 13 for information.

✔ If you don't remember someone's phone number, use the dialpad (refer to Figure 4-1) to type the person's name. Use the letter keys associated with each number on the dialpad to type the name; the Droid 4 is smart enough to display potential matches.

✔ The Call in Progress notification icon (refer to Figure 4-2) is useful. When you see this notification, the phone is connected to another party. To return to the phone screen, swipe down the status bar and touch the phone call's notification. You can then press the End Call button to disconnect or just put the phone to your face to see who's on the line.

Dialing an international number

You can use your Droid 4 to dial any phone number in the world, providing you know that number. (You might also want to know whose number you're calling and how to speak that person's language.) All international numbers you dial must be prefixed with a *country exit code*. To dial that code, press and hold the 0 (zero) key on the phone's dialpad until you see a + (plus sign) on the screen. You can then type the rest of the international number. For example, to dial Hong Kong, you press and hold the 0 key to get the + character, then dial 852, the international code for Hong Kong.

The + character effectively replaces the country exit code you would normally dial when calling internationally. In the United States, the country exit code is 011, so when you see an international number prefixed by 011, replace 011 with a + when dialing internationally on your Droid 4.

Only use the + character as a prefix; do not use it as a number separator. Also, be aware of international dialing surcharges. Verizon has a feature called I-Dial that you can add to your cell phone plan for frequent international callers. For more information on I-Dial, call 800-922-0204.

Dialing a contact

You can use the Droid 4's address book to quickly summon a contact and dial the contact's number. It's cinchy:

1. **At the Home screen, touch the Phone app icon.**

2. **Touch the Contacts tab at the top of the screen.**

3. **Scroll the list of contacts to find the person you want to call.**

   To find a contact, you can touch the first letter of the person's name on the right side of the screen. Or you can swipe your finger along the right side of the screen to rapidly scroll the list.

4. **Touch the contact you want to call.**

5. **Touch the green phone icon next to the phone number you want to dial.**

   The contact is dialed immediately.

At this point, dialing proceeds as described earlier in the chapter.

Phoning someone you call often

The Droid 4 keeps a record of your phone calls. That record, or *call log,* includes all the calls you've made, incoming calls, and even missed calls. You can quickly phone someone you call often by plucking the person's name from the call log, or you can use the call log to return a call you've missed. Obey these steps:

1. **Touch the Phone app on the Home screen.**

2. **Touch the Recent tab, found at the top of the window (refer to Figure 4-1).**

   The Recent tab displays a list of calls made, received, and missed. You can choose an item to see more information

3. **Touch the green phone icon next to the entry.**

   The phone dials the number.

You can access people you call frequently or contacts you've added to the Favorites list by touching the Favorites tab (refer to Figure 4-1). Scroll the list to find a favorite contact, or look at frequent contacts below the list of favorites, and then touch the green phone icon to dial.

See Chapter 5 for information on how to make one of your contacts a favorite.

Making a conference call

As a human being, you may not be able to hold two conversations at once, but your Droid 4 is up to the task. Your phone can call two people in a process called *making a conference call.* Here's how it works:

1. **Phone the first person.**

2. **After your phone connects and you complete a few pleasantries, touch the Add Call button.**

   Refer to Figure 4-2 for the location of the Add Call button. After you touch that button, the first person is put on hold. You now need to add the second person.

3. **Dial the second person.**

   You can use the dialpad or choose the second person from the phone's address book or one of the recent calls in the call log.

4. **Say your pleasantries and inform the party that the call is about to be merged.**

5. **Touch the Merge button.**

   The two calls are now joined. The touchscreen says *In Call* and the contact icon changes to show multiple silhouettes. These visual clues tell you that you're making a conference call. The audible clue is that everyone you've dialed can talk to and hear everyone else.

6. **To end the conference call, touch the End Call button.**

   All calls are disconnected.

When several people are in a room and want to participate in a call, you can always put the phone in speaker mode by touching the Speaker button.

It's For You!

Nothing can confirm your value to the universe like getting a phone call. It's far more significant than getting tagged in a Facebook update. Who cares if the caller is a telemarketer or a bill collector? The point is: The person cared enough to call. This section explains how to answer incoming calls on your Droid 4.

Receiving a call

Several things can happen when you receive a phone call on your Droid 4:

- ✐ The phone makes a noise signaling an incoming call.
- ✐ The phone vibrates.
- ✐ The touchscreen reveals information about the call, as shown in Figure 4-3.
- ✐ Your plucky assistant explains that the bomb squad is still several minutes away and you'll have to defuse the stolen nuke yourself using only Wikipedia as a reference.

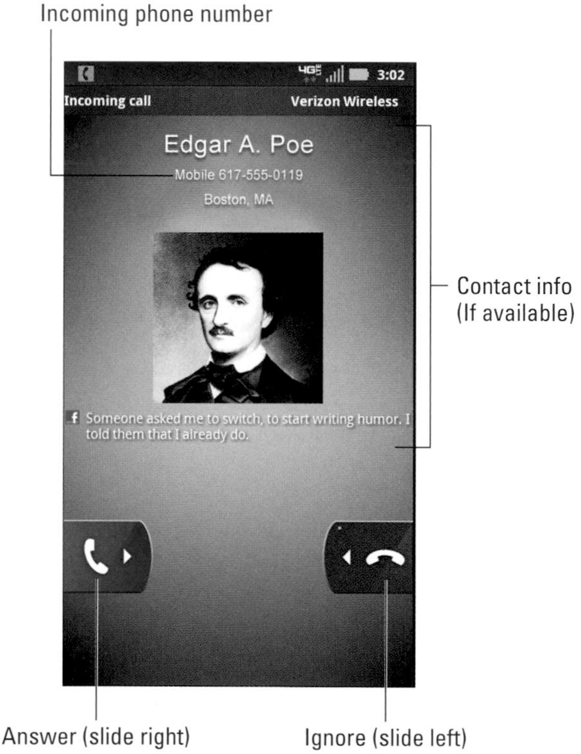

Incoming phone number

Answer (slide right)   Ignore (slide left)

Figure 4-3: You have an incoming call.

The last item in the list happens only in cheesy Hollywood movies. The other three possibilities, or a combination thereof, are your signals that you have an incoming call. A simple look at the touchscreen tells you more information, as illustrated in Figure 4-3.

To answer the incoming call, slide the green answer button to the right. Then place the phone to your ear. Say "Hello" or, if you're in a grouchy mood, say "What?" loudly.

To dispense with the incoming call, slide the red ignore button to the left. The phone stops ringing and the call is banished into voice mail.

If you're already using the phone when a call comes in, such as browsing the web or playing *Cut the Rope,* the incoming call screen looks subtly different from the one shown in Figure 4-3. Your choices for what to do with the call, however, are the same: Touch the green answer button to accept the call or touch the red ignore button to send the caller to voice mail.

- ✔ Missed calls are flagged by a Missed Call notification, as shown in the margin. Pull down the notifications to see who called, or choose the missed call notification to review missed calls in the call log.

- ✔ Calls that you dismiss (by sliding the red button to the left) are not counted as missed calls in the Droid 4's call log.

- ✔ You can silence the phone's incoming call noise by touching the Volume button on the side of the phone. Doing so doesn't dismiss the call; you can still choose to answer or ignore the call after muting the ringer.

- ✔ The contact's picture, such as Mr. Poe's in Figure 4-3, appears only when you've assigned a picture to that contact. Otherwise, the generic Android icon shows up. The contact's social networking information may also appear, depending on whether or not the contact is one of your social networking pals and you're currently logged into a social networking app on your Droid 4.

- ✔ If you're using a Bluetooth headset, you touch the control on the headset to answer your phone. See Chapter 13 for more information on using Bluetooth gizmos.

- ✔ The sound you hear when the phone rings is known as the *ringtone.* You can configure your phone to play a number of ringtones, depending on who is calling, or you can set a universal ringtone. Ringtones are covered in Chapter 15.

Receiving a new call when you're on the phone

You're on the phone, chatting it up, when someone else calls you. What happens next?

Your phone alerts you to the new call. The phone may vibrate or make a sound. Look at the front of the phone to see which number is calling and, if available, contact information. The text *Call Waiting* appears at the top of the screen, which tells you that the incoming call is awaiting your attention. You have three options:

- ✓ **Answer the call.** Touch the green answer button to answer the incoming call. The call you're on is placed on hold.

- ✓ **Send the call directly to voice mail.** Touch the red ignore button. The incoming call is sent directly to voice mail.

- ✓ **Do nothing.** The call eventually goes into voice mail.

As mentioned, when you choose to answer the call, the call you're on is placed on hold. You return to the first call when you end the second call. Or you can manage the multiple calls as described in the next section.

Juggling two calls

After you answer a second call, as described in the preceding section, your phone is working with two calls at a time. In this particular situation, you can speak with only one person at a time; juggling two calls isn't the same thing as a conference call, which is covered earlier in this chapter.

You can do a few things while the phone is handling two calls:

- ✓ **Switch between callers.** Touch the Switch Calls button that appears on the touchscreen. Every time you touch that button, the conversation moves to the other caller. The current person is then put on hold.

- ✓ **End a call.** Touch the End Call button, just as you normally do.

After ending one of the calls, the conversation returns back to the other caller. It may appear as though the phone has disconnected, but that's not the case: Wait a few moments and your phone rings, which is merely the way the phone system reconnects you with the previous call.

> ✔ The number of different calls your phone can handle depends on your carrier. For Verizon in the United States, your phone can handle only two calls at a time. In that case, a third person who calls you either hears a busy signal or is sent directly into voice mail.
>
> ✔ If the person on hold hangs up, you may hear a sound or feel the phone vibrate when the call is dropped.

Call Forwarding Options

Sometimes calls just aren't welcome, such as those from a pest or ones that really need to go elsewhere. For example, you might want to have calls forwarded from your business phone to your personal phone when you're on vacation. Or maybe you want unanswered calls sent to a voice mail service such as Google Voice. The various call forwarding options for the Droid 4 are covered in this section.

Forwarding phone calls

The job of call forwarding on your Droid 4 is handled by your cellular provider, Verizon, not by a software feature on the phone itself. The method, which works the same on every Verizon phone, requires you to dial a special number for call forwarding, as shown in Table 4-1.

Table 4-1	Verizon Call Forwarding Commands	
To Do This	*Input First Number*	*Input Second Number*
Forward unanswered incoming calls	*71	Forwarding number
Forward all incoming calls	*72	Forwarding number
Cancel call forwarding	*73	None

So, to forward all calls to 714-555-4565, you open the Phone app, type ***727145554565**, and touch the green phone button. You hear just a brief tone after dialing, and then the call ends. After that, any call coming into your phone rings at the other number.

📋 Forwarding all incoming calls (*72) works until you disable it. Your phone won't even ring when calls are forwarded.

📋 You use the *71 command to forward your unanswered calls to a voice mail service, such as Google Voice.

📋 If you do use Google Voice, be aware that cancelling call forwarding (*73) also disables Google Voice. You'll have to reenable Google Voice for your phone, per the directions offered on the Google Voice home page on the web.

📋 You must disable call forwarding to return to normal cell phone operations. Dial *73.

Sending a contact directly to voice mail

You can configure the Droid 4 to forward any of your cell phone contacts directly to voice mail. This feature is an ideal way to deal with a pest! Follow these steps:

1. **Touch the Apps icon on the Home screen.**

2. **Open the Contacts app.**

   You need to access the phone's address book.

3. **Choose a contact.**

   Use your finger to scroll the list of contacts until you find the annoying person you want to eternally banish to voice mail.

4. **Press the Menu soft button.**

5. **Choose Options.**

6. **Touch the square next to the Incoming Calls option.**

   A green check mark appears in the square, indicating that all calls from the contact (no matter which phone number the person uses) are sent directly into voice mail.

To un-banish the contact, repeat these steps but in Step 6 touch the square to remove the green check mark.

📋 This feature is one reason you might want to retain contact information for someone with whom you never want to have contact.

📋 See Chapter 5 for more information on the Droid 4's address book.

The Joy of Voice Mail

The most basic, and most stupid, form of voice mail is the free voice mail service provided by your cell phone company. This standard feature has few frills and nothing stands out differently, which is sad because the Droid 4 is an exceptional phone.

A wonderful alternative to boring, carrier voice mail is Google Voice. Refer to my book *Android Phones For Dummies* to learn more about setting up and using Google Voice as your Droid 4's voice mail system.

Setting up carrier voice mail

You need to set up voice mail on your phone. I recommend doing so, even if you plan on using another voice mail service, such as Google Voice, because carrier voice mail remains a valid and worthy fallback when those other services don't work.

Even if you believe that voice mail is set up and configured, consider churning through these steps, just to be sure:

1. **At the Home screen, press the Menu soft button.**
2. **Choose Settings.**

   The Settings screen appears.

3. **Choose Call Settings and then Voicemail Service.**
4. **Choose My Carrier, if it isn't chosen already.**

   Or, if it's the only option, you're set.

You can use the Voicemail Settings command to confirm or change the voice mail phone number. (You'll have to check with your cell phone carrier to see what the number is, though the proper number is most likely already input.)

After performing the steps in this section, call into the carrier voice mail service to finish the setup: Set your name, a voice mail password, a greeting, and various other steps as guided by your cellular provider's cheerful robot.

- The voice mail number for Verizon phones such as your Droid 4 is *86.
- The Droid 4 comes with a Voicemail app, though it's not really that fancy.

- ✓ I don't recommend using the Visual Voice Mail service offered by Verizon. It's not that expensive, but Google Voice is far better and won't cost you a nickel.

- ✓ Complete your voice mailbox setup by creating a customized greeting. If you don't, you may not receive voice mail messages, or people may believe that they've dialed the wrong number.

Retrieving your messages

When you have voice mail looming, the New Voicemail notification icon appears on the status bar, similar to the one shown in the margin. Tap this notification to connect to the voice mail service and deal with your messages.

The first thing you'll do when connected to Verizon voice mail is enter your PIN or password. My advice is to look at the phone so that you can see the dialpad, and also touch the Speaker button so that you can hear the prompts.

If you make a mistake when typing the password, press the * button and input your password again.

The Verizon voice mail system automatically plays any new or unheard messages.

To delete the message you just heard, press the 7 key. You can press the 7 key any time a message is playing to delete it.

When you're done with Verizon Voicemail, press the * key to end your session and hang up.

Chapter 5

The Address Book

*T*oss away that little black book. Forget about keeping names and addresses on 3-by-5 cards. And definitely stop writing phone numbers on the kitchen cabinet. Your Droid 4 comes with a complete, thorough, and well-integrated address book that keeps track of names, phone numbers, e-mail addresses, locations, and details intimate enough to embarrass even your closest friends.

Your Contacts

Although I would prefer the name Address Book, the Contacts app is where you'll find the people in your phone. That app, along with all the other apps on your Droid 4, is on the App menu. You can see the phone's address book also by opening the Phone app and touching the Contacts tab at the top of the screen.

Perusing the address book

The Contacts app appears as shown in Figure 5-1. The list of contacts is sorted alphabetically by first name, with the first name first. That order can be changed; see the later section "Sorting the address book."

Individual contact (no picture)   View contacts

View contact goups   Favorite contacts

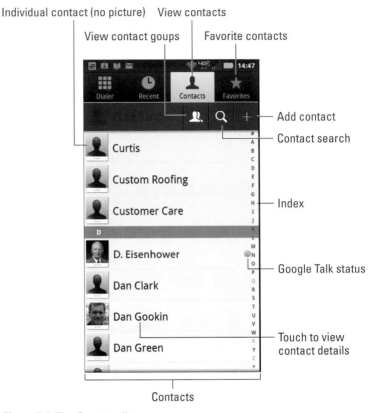

Add contact

Contact search

Index

Google Talk status

Touch to view
contact details

Contacts

Figure 5-1: The Contacts list.

Flip through the list by swiping your finger up or down. You can
use the index on the right side of the screen (refer to Figure 5-1) to
quickly scroll up and down through your contacts.

Viewing a contact's information

To get to a contact's details, you have to touch the contact's name
in the phone's address book, the Contacts app. The additional
information you see can be quite detailed, such as that shown in
Figure 5-2, or just a name and phone number. The amount of information depends on what you've entered for the contact.

Recent calls, texts, and e-mails

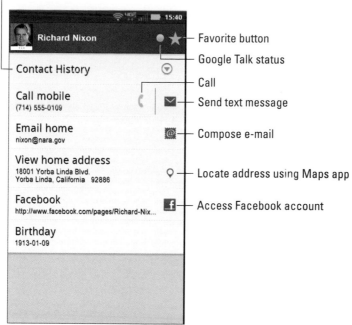

Figure 5-2: More detail about a contact.

You can do a multitude of things with the contact after it's displayed, as illustrated in Figure 5-2:

- **Make a phone call.** To call the contact, touch one of the contact's phone entries, such as Call Home or Call Mobile. You touch the entry itself, or touch the green phone icon by the entry.

- **Send a text message.** Touch the text message icon (see Figure 5-2) to open the Text app and send the contact a message. See Chapter 6 for information about text messaging.

- **Compose an e-mail message.** Touch the compose e-mail icon to type an e-mail message to the contact. When the contact has more than one e-mail address, you can choose to which one you want to send the message. Chapter 6 covers using e-mail on your phone.

- **Locate your contact on a map.** When the contact has a home or business address, you can touch the little doohickey next to the address (labeled in Figure 5-2), to summon the Maps application. Refer to my book, *Android Phones For Dummies*, to see all the fun stuff you can do with the Maps app.

    ✔ **View social networking info.** Visit the contact's Facebook, Twitter, or another social networking account by touching the appropriate item. See Chapter 8 for additional information on social networking with your Droid 4.

As mentioned, the amount of information you see, depends on what you entered for the contact. The more information, the more you can do with a contact.

    ✔ Your own account on the Droid 4 is called Me. You may also have an entry under your own name, though the Me account is created when you first set up your phone.

    ✔ When you're done viewing the contact's details, press the Back soft button.

    ✔ Social networking information appears only if you've configured your Droid 4 with your social networking account information and you're logged in to the proper social networking app on your phone.

    ✔ Information about your contacts is pulled from multiple sources: your Google account, the phone's storage, and your social networking sites. When you see duplicated information for a contact, the information probably comes from two or more of those sources.

    ✔ Weird people named #BAL, #DATA, or Customer Care are not real contacts but shortcuts to various services offered by your cellular provider. For example, the #BAL contact is used to get a free text message listing your current account balance.

Sorting the address book

You don't have to tolerate how names are listed by the Contacts app. If you prefer to see the list sorted last name first, you can change the order. If you prefer the list to be presented last name first instead of first name first, you can change that, too. Follow these steps in the Contacts app:

1. **Press the Menu soft button and choose Display Options.**

2. **Choose Sort List By.**

3. **Select First Name or Last Name to sort the list accordingly.**

   After making the selection, you're returned to the Display Options screen.

4. **Choose View Contact Names As.**

5. **Select either First Name First or Last Name First to specify how contacts are displayed in the list.**

   The way the names are displayed doesn't affect the way the names are sorted. For example, if you selected Last Name for the sort order and First Name First as the display order, the list remains sorted by last name.

6. **Touch the Save button to lock in your choices.**

The Contacts list is updated, displayed per your preferences.

Searching for your friends

Sure, you can drag your finger up and down the index to quickly find a contact, but that method becomes unwieldy when you have hundreds of contacts. A better option is to touch the Search soft button to display the Contact Search screen. Type all or part of a contact's name and you see the list of contacts narrowed to the few who match the letters you type. Touch a name from the search list to view that contact's information.

More Friends for You

Who couldn't use some more friends? When you encounter a new pal or phone number you need to keep, you can add it to the Droid 4 address book. How, you ask? You can try mental telepathy to get the new contact information into the phone. You can try physically pressing the phone against the new contact. Or you can rely upon the helpful information in this section.

Details about your social networking friends can be merged into the address book whenever you add social networking sites to your Android phone. See Chapter 8 for details on social networking.

Adding a contact from the call log

The fastest way I've found to add a new contact to my phone is to use the list of recent callers, what I refer to as the *call log*. After someone phones me, if I don't already have the caller's information in the phone, I add the person's name and phone number by obeying these quick, few steps:

1. **Open the Phone app.**

2. **Touch the Recent tab at the top of the screen.**

3. **Choose the phone number from the list of recent calls.**

4. **Choose Add to Contacts.**

   If the number belongs to an existing contact, you'd choose the contact from the list. For these steps, we're adding a new contact.

5. **Choose Create New Contact.**

6. **Choose your Google account for the location to store the new contact.**

   By choosing your Google account, you ensure that the contact's information is duplicated from your Droid 4 to your Google account on the Internet. In fact, I recommend that you touch the gray square by the item Remember This Choice so that you're not prompted again.

   If you see other account options, such as Yahoo or Hotmail, you can choose those locations for saving the new contact information instead of Google. Your choice depends on which Internet service you use as your primary e-mail account or address book.

7. **Touch OK.**

8. **Fill in the contact's information.**

   Fill in as many blanks as you can. If you fill in only the name, you'll still be clued in to who is calling the next time that person calls (using the same number).

   I recommend that you add the area code prefix to the phone number, if it's not automatically added for you.

9. **Touch the Save button to create the new contact.**

One of the location options for saving the contact information is Verizon Backup Assistant. I don't bother with Backup Assistant, mostly because I've never tried it and also because I find the Google services easy to use.

Creating a new contact from scratch

When you meet someone new and want to put the person's information into your phone, you'll need to do a bit of typing. Sure, you could have the person phone you right there, and then follow the steps in the preceding section. But often it's just quicker — and less awkward — to follow these steps:

1. **Open the Contacts app.**

2. **Press the Menu soft button and choose the Add Contact command.**

   There may also be an Add Contact button found near the top of the screen.

3. **If prompted, choose your Google account as the place to store the contact and then touch the OK button.**

   I recommend choosing Google, unless you use another account listed, such as Yahoo!

4. **On the Add Contact screen, fill in the information as the contact begrudgingly recites it.**

   Fill in the text fields with the information you know, such as the first and last names.

   To add an item, such as a second phone number, touch the green plus button next to that item, as shown in Figure 5-3.

   Touch a gray button to the left of the phone number to choose whether it's the home, work, or mobile number. Do the same for the contact's e-mail address.

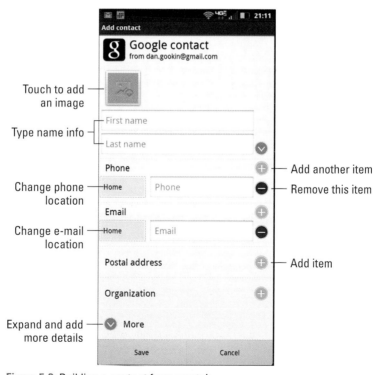

Figure 5-3: Building a contact from scratch.

Touch the More button at the bottom of the list to expand that area and add *even more* information!

5. **Touch the Save button to add the new contact.**

You can create new contacts also by using your Gmail account on a computer. This option offers you the luxury of using a full-size keyboard and computer screen. However, whenever you meet a contact face-to-face, creating the contact using your phone will have to suffice.

Finding a new contact by location

You can use a trick with the Maps app to easily add a business contact to your Droid 4. Whenever you use the Maps app to locate a restaurant, a haberdashery, or an apothecary, you can create an address book entry for that location by heeding these steps:

1. **Open the Maps app.**

   The Maps app is found on the Apps menu, along with all the other apps on your Droid 4.

2. **Search for a business or other location using the Maps app.**

   Touch the Search Maps text box and then type what you're looking for, such as *Italian Restaurant* or *Movie Theater*. The Maps app displays the results on the screen, highlighting nearby locations.

3. **If the marker you're interested in doesn't sport a cartoon bubble, touch that marker, highlighting its location on the map.**

   The cartoon bubble shows information about that location, as shown in Figure 5-4.

Figure 5-4: Finding a location on the map.

4. **Touch the cartoon bubble to see more information.**

5. **Choose the item Add as Contact.**

   You'll have to scroll down the list of information to find the Add as Contact button.

6. **If prompted, choose in which account to store the contact, then touch OK.**

   The information for the business, including the address and phone number, is copied into the proper fields.

7. **Touch the Save button.**

   The new contact is created.

For more information on the Maps app, refer to my book, *Android Phones For Dummies* (Wiley).

Address Book Management

I don't know how many times I hear people panic about getting a new phone number or e-mail address. They almost react as if it's more upsetting than moving. But things change, and occasionally you'll need to update the information in the Contacts app to account for new information. This section shows you how.

Making basic changes

To make minor touch-ups on any contact, start by locating and displaying the contact's information. Press the Menu soft button and choose the Edit Contact command.

The contact's information is displayed, organized by source: Google contact information, information culled from social networking sites, plus information drawn from other sources, if any.

Change, add, or edit information by touching a field and typing the new details.

Some information cannot be edited. For example, fields pulled in from social networking sites can be edited only by that account holder on the social networking site.

When you're done editing, touch the Save button.

In case of emergency . . .

An account at the top of the Contacts list is titled In Case of Emergency. This account, which has a big red plus icon by its name, is not really an address book account, but rather a place where you can fill in emergency contact information and other vital information. That way, should you become injured or incapacitated, a public safety official or helpful bystander can pick up your phone to get emergency information about you.

To make the In Case of Emergency information useful, choose that item on your phone. If the fields are empty, press the Menu soft button and choose the Edit command. Type your name into the Assign Owner field. Choose an ICE (In Case of Emergency) field and then pluck out a contact from the address book to assign to that field.

You can also fill in the Emergency Notes fields with vital information, such as allergies, relevant medical history, insurance information, your religious preferences, or your favorite type of music.

Touch the Save button when you're done configuring the emergency contact information.

Adding a picture to a contact

It's nice to have an image associated with a contact. The image appears not only by the contact's name in the Droid 4's address book but also on the screen when you make a call to or receive a call from that person. You can assign the image using the Droid 4 when you edit the contact's information. Sometimes the image is automatically pulled from a social networking site.

To add or change the image, follow these steps:

1. **Locate and display the contact's information.**

2. **Press the Menu soft button and choose the Edit Contact command.**

3. **Touch the icon where the contact's picture would go, or touch the existing picture assigned to the contact.**

    The icon shows a generic placeholder if no picture is assigned, as shown in Figure 5-3.

4. **If you're changing an existing contact image, choose the Change Photo command.**

5. **Choose the option Select Photo from Gallery.**

   If you have another image management app installed on your Droid 4, you can choose that app from the list instead of choosing the Gallery. Or if you see a Complete Action Using prompt, choose the My Gallery app.

6. **Browse the gallery to look for a suitable image.**

   See Chapter 9 for more information on using the Gallery.

7. **Touch the image you want to use for the contact.**

   The image is assigned and will appear whenever the contact is referenced on your phone.

8. **Touch the Save button to save the changes for that contact.**

You can add pictures to contacts on your Google account by using any computer. Just visit your Gmail Contacts list to edit a contact. You can then add to that contact any picture stored on your computer. The picture is eventually synced with the same contact on your Droid 4 phone.

✔ To remove or change a contact's picture, in Step 4 choose the Remove Photo command.

✔ Some images in the Gallery may not work for contact icons. For example, images synchronized with your online photo albums may be unavailable.

Making a favorite

A *favorite* contact is someone you stay in touch with most often. The person doesn't have to be someone you like — just someone you (perhaps unfortunately) phone often, such as your bookie.

The list of favorite contacts is kept on the Phone app's Favorites tab (refer to Figure 5-1). The top part of the list shows favorite favorites, or those contacts you've flagged with a star icon, specifically designating them as a favorite. Below those favorites are a list of people you contact frequently but who are not (yet) favorites — ideal candidates for promotion to the Favorites list.

To add a contact to the Favorites list, display the contact's information and touch the star button in the contact's upper-right corner. When the star is green (refer to Figure 5-2), the contact is one of your favorites.

To remove a favorite, touch the contact's star again and it loses its color. Removing a favorite doesn't delete the contact but instead removes it from the Favorites list.

> ✔ You do not have to edit the contact before setting the favorite status.
>
> ✔ The contact has no idea whether they're one of your favorites, so don't believe that you're hurting anyone's feelings by not making them a favorite. Again, favorites are simply contacts you phone frequently; you don't have to like them.

Joining contacts

When it comes to recognizing one person with two entries in the Droid 4's address book, the Contacts app tries to be smart by joining the contacts, into one entry.

Then again, sometimes the Contacts app isn't quite that smart and it overlooks some duplicate contacts. To merge, or *join,* two separate contacts, follow these steps:

1. **Open the Contacts app and display one of the duplicate contacts.**

2. **Press the Menu soft button.**

3. **Choose the Join command.**

   If you don't see the Join command, choose More, choose Join.

4. **Choose the second contact from the list displayed.**

   The Droid 4 may guess, displaying some contacts it believes match the one you selected. If so, you'll see a list of suggested contacts. If the contact you want isn't in the list, choose the option Show All Contacts.

   When the Droid 4 can't find any matches, the entire contact list is displayed.

5. **Choose the duplicate contact.**

   Both contacts are joined.

If you'd like to test the Join command, choose your own contact information in Step 1. Then, in Step 4, choose the Me account. The Droid 4 creates that account to represent your own information, so joining the Me account with your personal account is possible.

Splitting contacts

Just as similar contacts can be joined, they can also be torn asunder. The command, however, is not called Tear Asunder. It's called Separate or Split, depending on where you find it.

The Droid 4 can and does join what it believes to be similar address book contacts. (See the preceding section.) Sometimes it boo-boos and joins two contacts who are not the same person. For example, I have Facebook friends who are also named Dan Gookin, and yet the Droid 4 seems to think we're all one guy.

To separate an improperly joined contact, summon the contact on the Droid 4 and press the Menu soft button. Choose the Split or Separate command. If you don't see the command, touch the More button, then choose Split or Separate. Touch the OK button to confirm.

Lo: From whence there was one, there are now two!

Removing a contact

Every so often, consider reviewing your phone's contacts. Purge those folks whom you no longer recognize, have forgotten, or despise. It's simple:

1. **Locate the contact in your phone's address book and display the contact's information.**

2. **Press the Menu soft button and choose the command Delete Contact.**

   A warning may appear, depending on whether the contact has information linked from your social networking sites. If so, dismiss the warning by touching the OK button.

3. **Touch OK to remove the contact from your phone.**

When the contact source is Google (your Gmail account), the contact is removed from the Internet as well. Likewise, when purging a contact you've saved in, say, your Yahoo! account, the contact is removed from that online account as well. Be careful what you delete!

Chapter 6

Messages In and Out

· ·

· ·

There may come a time when making phone calls isn't your first choice for communications on a cell phone. And that time may arrive sooner than you think: For the younger crowd, text messaging is now more popular than talking. My son's cell phone records show maybe 14 minutes of calls every month but thousands of text messages. Stir in the Droid 4's capability to do e-mail, and you have an entire chapter full of nonverbal communication methods, one of which may soon eclipse talking.

Message Central

Communicating with text is as old as the alphabet. Electronic text communications is about 150 years old, dating back to the telegraph. Your Droid 4 lacks the capability to work as a telegraph, so you can ease your mind about learning Morse code. But knowing that your phone can handle text communications in several ways does help. This section offers an overview.

Adding e-mail accounts

Your Droid 4 can deftly handle all your e-mail duties. It can receive and send electronic messages, deal with attachments, forward messages — all that jazz. Nothing can happen, however, until you set up your e-mail accounts on the phone. Follow these steps:

1. **Open the My Accounts app.**

   The app is found on the App menu.

2. **Touch the Add Account button.**

3. **Choose the Email Accounts icon.**

   If you're adding a corporate account, such as your organization's internal e-mail account, choose the Corporate Sync item.

4. **If you see your account, such as AOL, Yahoo!, or Windows Live Hotmail, choose that icon. Otherwise, choose the Other icon.**

5. **Type your account's e-mail address.**

6. **Type the password for the account.**

7. **Touch the Next button.**

   In a few magical moments, the e-mail account is configured and added to the account list.

   If you goofed up the account name or password, you're warned: Try again.

8. **Touch the Done button.**

   The account is added to the list on the My Accounts screen.

You can repeat the steps in this section to add more e-mail accounts.

✔ If you see an error message when setting up an ISP account, you need to manually configure the connection. After you see the error message, touch the Set Up Manually button. On the next screen, choose each of the three available categories: General Settings, Incoming Server, and Outgoing Server. Use information provided by your ISP to fill in the details.

✔ Your ISP most likely has information on its website for configuring Android phones, such as the Droid 4. Check with your ISP for details.

✔ Your Gmail account is already configured for your Droid 4. Even so, you can add more Gmail accounts using the techniques in this section, should you have multiple Gmail accounts.

Accessing your messages

Rather than stumble and fumble to find new messages on the Droid 4, you can visit a single app. It's called the Messaging app, and it's shown in Figure 6-1.

The Messaging app pulls in messages from multiple sources and displays them all in one place. The sources include text messaging, all the e-mail accounts you've set up, and even social networking sites. To read your new messages, simply touch a source icon, such as Main shown in Figure 6-1. To read all your new messages — even text messages — touch the Universal Inbox (also shown in Figure 6-1).

  ✔ New messages for an account are noted by a number shown in a blue bubble.

  ✔ The later section "Reading an e-mail message" discusses how to read e-mail received on your Droid 4.

  ✔ The Messaging app doesn't list your Gmail account. Gmail is part of the Google pantheon of apps, so it's treated separately.

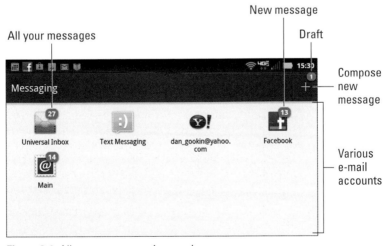

New message

All your messages   Draft

Compose new message

Universal Inbox   Text Messaging   dan_gookin@yahoo.   Facebook
                                          com

Various e-mail accounts

Main

Figure 6-1: All your messages, in one place.

Using specific messaging apps

The Messaging app serves as a central location for all incoming messages — text, e-mail, and social networking — in your phone. To compose messages, you can use specific apps for each type of service. For reading and composing text messages, use the Text Messaging app. See the section "The Joy of Text."

For reading and composing Gmail, use the Gmail app, which hooks directly into your Google Gmail account. In fact, they're echoes of each other: The Gmail you receive on your computer is received also on your phone.

For reading and composing all other types of e-mail, use the Email app. That app is used to connect to non-Gmail electronic mail, such as the standard mail service provided by your ISP or a web-based e-mail system such as Yahoo! Mail or Windows Live Mail.

- ✏ The Email app is configured to handle multiple e-mail accounts. See the earlier section "Adding e-mail accounts" for information on adding e-mail accounts to your Droid 4.

- ✏ Although you can use your phone's web browser to visit the Gmail website, you should use the Gmail app to pick up your Gmail.

- ✏ If you forget your Gmail password, visit www.google.com/accounts/ForgotPasswd

The Joy of Text

The common name for using your Droid 4 smartphone to send short, typed messages to another cell phone is *texting*. It's not just something for the under-25 crowd, either.

Texting comes in handy for short, quick, to-the-point communications. It's faster and less obtrusive than a phone call. And if you do have relatives under the age of 25, it's probably the only way you'll get them to communicate with you.

On the Droid 4, the app that handles texting is called Text Messaging. It appears on the Home screen, in the dock (at the bottom of the Home screen), and is named Text. I assume that the Messaging part of the app's full name is lurking somewhere below the touchscreen.

- ✏ Don't text while you're driving, in a movie theater, or in any situation where paying more attention to your phone than to your surroundings is awkward or inappropriate.

- ✏ Your cellular service plan may charge you per message for every text message you send. Some plans feature a given number of free (included) messages per month. Other plans, favored by teenagers (and their parents), feature unlimited texting.

✔ The nerdy term for text messaging is *SMS*, which stands for Short Message Service.

Composing a text message

Because most cell phones sport a text-messaging feature, you can send a text message to just about any mobile number. The process works like this:

1. **Open the Text Messaging app.**

2. **If the app opens to a specific conversation, press the Back soft button to return to the main screen.**

   The main screen lists all your text message conversations.

3. **If you see the person you want to text listed as one of the conversations, touch that entry on the screen. Otherwise, touch the green plus button to compose a new text message.**

4. **Type the phone number to text or type a contact's name.**

   As you type, any matching contacts appear in a list; choose a contact to save yourself some typing time.

5. **You can optionally type additional people to text, in which case the message is sent to everyone you specify.**

   Normally, you text only one person at a time.

6. **Touch the Compose Message field and type the text message.**

   Be brief. A text message has a 160-character limit. You can check the screen to see whether you're nearing the limit, as shown in Figure 6-2.

7. **Touch the Send button.**

   The message is sent instantly. Whether the contact replies instantly depends.

8. **When the person replies, read the displayed message.**

9. **Repeat Steps 6 through 8 as needed — or eternally, whichever comes first.**

You don't need to continually look at your phone while waiting for a text message. When your contact chooses to reply, the message is recorded as part of an ongoing conversation. See the later section "Receiving a text message."

Any previous conversation appears here

The contact you're texting   Number of characters left to type

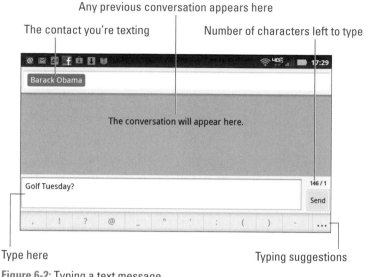

Type here   Typing suggestions

Figure 6-2: Typing a text message.

 ✔ You can easily compose a text message to a contact when you summon that contact's screen in the Contacts app. Touch the Message icon, shown in the margin, next to the contact's phone number to compose a text message to that number.

 ✔ You can send text messages only to cell phones. Aunt Carol cannot receive text messages on her landline that she's had since the 1960s.

✔ Continue a conversation at any time: Open the phone's texting app, peruse the list of existing conversations, and touch one to review what has been said or to pick up the conversation.

 ✔ Do not text and drive. Do not text and drive. Do not text and drive.

Receiving a text message

 When a new text message comes in, it appears briefly at the top of the phone's touchscreen. Then you see the New Text Message notification, similar to what's shown in the margin.

To view the message, pull down the notifications, as described in Chapter 3. Touch the messaging notification and that conversation window immediately opens.

 When you send a message to multiple people, you can reply to them all by touching the Send To All button when composing your reply

Forwarding a text message

It's possible to forward a text message, but it's not the same as forwarding e-mail. In fact, when it comes to forwarding information, e-mail has text messaging beat by well over 160 characters.

When forwarding works as an option, your phone lets you forward only the information in a text-messaging cartoon bubble, not the entire conversation. Here's how it works:

1. **If necessary, open a conversation in the Text Messaging app.**

2. **Long-press the text entry (the cartoon bubble) you want to forward.**

3. **From the menu that appears, choose the command Forward Message.**

   From this point on, forwarding the message works like sending a new message from scratch.

4. **Type the recipient's name (if the person is a contact) or type a phone number.**

   The text you're forwarding appears, already written, in the text field.

5. **Touch the Send button to forward the message.**

Attaching media to a text message

You can send a picture, a video, music, or other media with a text message, contrary to its nickname. Doing so creates a *multimedia message*. The good news is that attaching media is simple. The better news is that you can use the same Text Messaging app to accomplish that task.

The trick works like this:

1. **Compose a message like you normally would, as described earlier in this chapter.**

2. **Press the Menu soft button.**

3. **Choose the Insert command.**

   A menu appears listing a whole slew of things you can stick into a text message. The variety depends on the apps installed on your phone, though traditionally the items Existing Picture or Existing Video are the most popular.

When you choose a New item, such as New Picture or New Video, you can use the Droid 4 as a camera to capture an image or a video for an instant attachment.

4. **If prompted, choose the app from which you'll pluck the media.**

5. **Optionally edit the media.**

   For example, you might see a warning that the picture or video is too large. If so, touch the Resize button to make it more suitable as a multimedia text message attachment

6. **Touch the Send button to send off the media.**

In just a few, short, cellular moments, the receiving party will enjoy your multimedia text message.

✔ An easier way to send a multimedia message is to start with the source, such as a picture or video stored on your phone. Use the Share command or button (refer to the icon in the margin) and choose Text Messaging to share that media item.

✔ Not every phone is capable of receiving multimedia messages. Rather than receive the media item, the recipient may be directed to a web page where the item can be viewed on the Internet.

✔ The official name for a multimedia text message is Multimedia Messaging Service, which is abbreviated MMS.

Setting the text message ringtone

There's no reason your Droid 4 should sport the same boring ringtone notification for when a new text message comes in. Why not spice things up a bit by following these steps:

1. **Open the Text Messaging app.**

2. **Ensure that you're viewing the main screen, which lists all your conversations.**

   If you're not viewing that screen, press the Back soft button.

3. **Press the Menu soft button.**

4. **Choose the Messaging Settings command.**

5. **Choose Select Ringtone.**

6. **Pluck a ringtone from the list.**

7. **Touch the OK button.**

E-Mail on the Droid 4

Two apps on your Droid 4 deal with e-mail: The Gmail app and the Email app. They're both similar, handling the basic chores of e-mail: sending, receiving, forwarding, and otherwise managing your electronic messages as best as can be done on a cell phone. This section goes over the basics.

Refer to my book, *Android Phones For Dummies*, for additional information on customizing the e-mail experience on your Droid 4, including customizing your e-mail signature.

Getting a new message

Any e-mail that floats into your Droid 4 generates a notification. The notification icons differ, depending on the e-mail source. For example:

  ✔ New Gmail messages produce the New Gmail notification, as shown in the margin.

  ✔ New e-mail messages generate the New Email notification. This notification appears for whatever e-mail accounts you've set up, though some e-mail services (such as Yahoo! Mail) have their own icons.

  ✔ New Yahoo! Mail has its own notification icon, as shown in the margin.

You may see other specific mail notification icons as well, though the Gmail and Email notifications are the most common.

To deal with a new-message notification, drag down the notifications and choose the appropriate one. You're taken directly to your inbox to read the new message.

Reading an e-mail message

The way the message looks on your phone depends on whether you're using the Gmail or Email app. Figure 6-3 shows the Gmail interface; Figure 6-4 shows the Email apps message-reading interface.

From

Message subject   Star message   Show/hide toolbar

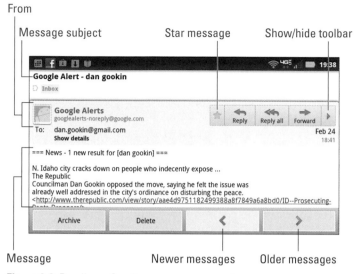

Message   Newer messages   Older messages

Figure 6-3: Reading a Gmail message on your phone.

Message content   Display boring information

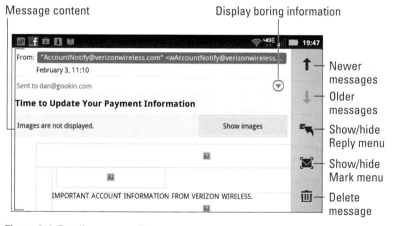

Newer messages

Older messages

Show/hide Reply menu

Show/hide Mark menu

Delete message

Figure 6-4: Reading an e-mail message.

Browse messages by touching the arrow buttons at the bottom of the message screen. The buttons may point left and right (refer to Figure 6-3) or up or down. That difference was created merely to confuse you.

Replying to the message works similarly to composing a new message in the Gmail or Email program. Refer to the next section.

Composing a new message

If you're familiar with creating e-mail on a computer, doing so on a phone won't seem much different. You use the Gmail app for composing new Gmail messages, and the Email app composes messages for whatever other e-mail services you use. The interface for both apps is similar, as shown in Figure 6-5.

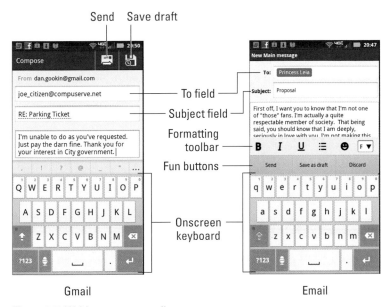

Figure 6-5: Writing a new e-mail message.

Here's how to create an e-mail message using your phone:

1. **Start an e-mail app, either Gmail or Email.**

   You may also be able to compose a new message from the Universal Inbox app (refer to Figure 6-1).

2. **In the Gmail app, press the Menu soft button and choose Compose; in the Email app, touch the green plus button.**

   A new message screen appears, looking similar to Figure 6-5 but with none of the fields filled in.

3. **If necessary, touch the To field to select it.**

4. **Type the first few letters of a contact name, and then choose a matching contact from the list that's displayed.**

   If the e-mail address isn't in your Contacts list, simply type the address.

5. **Type a subject.**

6. **Type the message.**

7. **Touch the Send button to instantly deliver your e-epistle.**

   In Gmail, you can touch the Save Draft button and the message is stored in the Drafts folder. You can open this folder to edit the message. Touch Send to send it.

Copies of messages you send in the Email app are stored in the Sent mailbox. If you're using Gmail, copies are saved in your Gmail account, which is accessed from your phone or from any computer connected to the Internet.

Chapter 7

Let's Talk

*W*hen it comes to communications, your Droid 4 does it all. Sure, it's a phone, but that means you can just talk, which can be boring. Text messaging is more immediate, and e-mail offers opportunities for composing long missives — but those are text-based communications. Better than all those options is video chat. It's the holy grail of telecommunications, and it's something your Droid 4 can do easily. So put on your clothes, grab your phone, and get ready to video chat.

Google Wants You to Talk

The key to video chat on any cell phone is that front-facing camera. With that in place, all your phone needs is a video chat app. On the Droid 4, that app is Google Talk.

Using Google Talk

You'll find the Google Talk app on your Droid 4, dwelling on the Apps menu. The app is listed as Talk, though the full name is Google Talk.

When you start the Talk app the first time, you'll be prompted to sign in using your Google account: Touch the Sign In button. I'm sure they could have made the setup more painful than that, but they chose not to.

After signing in, you'll see the main Talk screen, shown in Figure 7-1. Your Google contacts who have activated Google Talk, either on their computer or on a mobile gizmo like your Droid 4, are shown along with whether they're available to chat.

You can do three things with your friends while using the Talk app: text chat, voice chat, and video chat — the Holy Grail. But before you do any of that, you need to get some friends.

✔ Set your status by touching your account name at the top of the list (refer to Figure 7-1). You can also set a status message and tell others whether you're available for voice or video chat.

✔ To sign out of Google Talk, press the Menu soft button and choose the Sign Out command.

Friends list

Touch to set your status

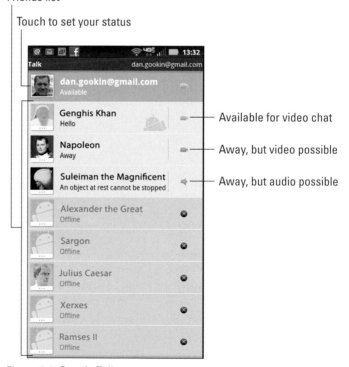

Available for video chat

Away, but video possible

Away, but audio possible

Figure 7-1: Google Talk.

Inviting a friend to Google Talk

You don't have any Google Talk friends? They'd be showing up on the Friends list in the Talk app. That problem can easily be fixed by heeding these steps in the Talk app:

1. **Press the Menu soft button.**

2. **Choose the Add Friend command.**

3. **Type your friend's name or e-mail address.**

   As you type, matches from your phone's address book appear in a list. Choose a friend from the list to instantly stuff his or her address into the text box.

4. **Touch the Send Invitation button.**

The best way for your pals to receive an invitation is for them to be using a mobile device running the Talk app or to be on a computer with the Gmail web page open. After they receive the invitation, they'll find it listed in their Friends list; Google Talk initiations have the heading Chat Invitation.

Your friends can be on a computer or mobile device to use Google Talk; it doesn't matter which. But they must have a camera available to video chat.

Typing at your friends

The most basic form of communications with the Talk app is text chatting. That means typing at another person, which is probably one of the oldest forms of communication on the Internet. Typing is also the most tedious, so I'll be brief.

Text chatting starts by touching a contact from the Friends list. Type your message as shown in Figure 7-2. Touch the Send button to send your comment.

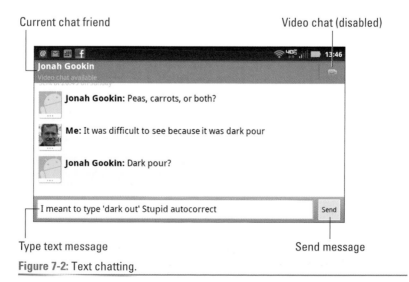

Current chat friend

Video chat (disabled)

Type text message

Send message

Figure 7-2: Text chatting.

You type, they type, and so on until you get tired or the phone runs out of battery juice.

When you're done talking, press the Menu soft button and choose the Friends List command to return to the main Talk screen (refer to Figure 7-1). You can just choose another friend from the list and chat with that person, or press the Home soft button to do something else with your phone.

Resume any conversation by choosing that same contact from the Friends list.

Talking and video chat

Take the conversation up a notch by touching the Video Chat button on the right side of the text chat window (refer to Figure 7-2). The camera icon (shown in the figure) means that video chat is available; a microphone icon indicates voice chat is available (not video); a round dot means text only.

 When you start a voice or video chat, your friend receives an invite pop-up and Talk notification on his or her Android phone. Or if a friend is asking you to voice or video chat, you'll see the pop-up. Touch the Accept button to begin talking.

Figure 7-3 shows a video chat. The person you're talking with appears in the big window; you're in the smaller window. With the connection made and the invite accepted, you can begin enjoying video chat.

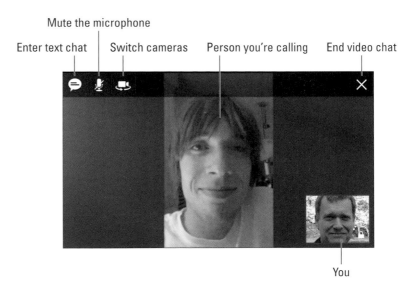

Mute the microphone

Enter text chat | Switch cameras | Person you're calling | End video chat

You

Figure 7-3: Video chat with Google Talk.

The controls atop the screen may vanish after a second; touch the screen to see the controls again.

To end the conversation, touch the X (close) button. Well, say "Goodbye" first, and then touch the X button.

> ✔ When you're nude, or just don't want to video chat, touch the Decline button for the video chat invite. Then choose that contact and reply with a text message or voice chat instead.

> ✔ You can disable incoming voice and video chats by deselecting the Allow Video and Voice Chats item on your Talk account's Status screen: At the main Talk screen, touch your account above the Friends list (refer to Figure 7-1).

> ✔ The Droid 4's front-facing camera is at the top right on the front of the phone. To make eye contact, look directly into the camera; note that you can't make eye contact and see the other person at the same time.

Other Ways to Stay in Touch

The Droid 4 comes with a two other apps that help you keep in touch with people: GoToMeeting and IM. Neither is as sexy as using video chat with Google Talk.

The GoToMeeting app allows you to hook your Droid 4 into the popular GoToMeeting service on the Internet. You can use the app to participate in online conferences, demonstrations, and even meetings. After starting the app, type the Meeting ID, your name, and optionally an e-mail address. Touch the Join Meeting button to participate in the meeting.

The IM in the IM app's name stands for Instant Messaging. It's the old Internet equivalent of text messaging, also known as a *chat room*. After starting the app, you'll see a list of your IM accounts. (If you don't see any, press the Menu soft button and choose Add Account.) IM works with AOL Instant Messenger (AIM), Yahoo!, and Windows Live Messenger.

I'll admit that I'm not really into IM, though if it's your passion you can use the IM app to sate your IM desires on your Droid 4.

> ✔ Yes, using the GoToMeeting app assumes that you've been invited to a meeting. That meeting must be configured and set up using GoToMeeting on a computer; you cannot use your Droid 4 to host a meeting.

✔ The IM app on your Droid 4 uses the cellular network whether or not the phone is connected to Wi-Fi. See Chapter 13 for more information on network communications.

Mobile Communications with Skype

Another popular way to communicate with others using your Droid 4 is to employ the Skype program. Skype is like the Internet's phone system: You can use Skype to place calls not only to other Skype users on the Internet but also to real phones. In fact, Skype is perhaps the most popular way to make international calls because it's so inexpensive.

 The Droid 4 doesn't come with a Skype app, but you can obtain one: Scan the QR code in the margin or visit the Play Store and pick up the Skype app or the Skype Mobile app.

You'll also need a Skype account to get the most from Skype. I recommend setting that account up on a computer connected to the Internet. Visit www.skype.com to get started. After you set up your Skype user name and password, you can use the Skype app on your Droid 4.

✔ Skype can be used for text chat, voice communications, and video chat.

✔ To use video chat with Skype, both phones must have a front-facing camera and the Skype app must be able to work with that camera. Not every smartphone with a front-facing camera can use the Skype app.

✔ Voice and video chat on Skype over the Internet is free. When you use a Wi-Fi connection, you can chat without incurring usage charges on your cellular plan's data minutes.

✔ Calls you place to phones with Skype cost money. You need to add Skype Credit to your account to place those calls. I recommend using a computer to log in to Skype on the Internet and then add Skype Credit.

✔ I've used Skype to place phone calls when I'm overseas. The cost to call home was only about 2¢ cents per minute, which is cheap. That's $1.20 to talk for an hour.

✔ If you plan to use Skype a lot, get a good headset.

✔ For more information on Skype, including building your Skype contacts list and details on placing calls, see my book *Android Phones For Dummies*.

Chapter 8

The Internet Experience

I don't need to convince you of the value of the Internet. In fact, you probably know the value every month when you get your cell phone bill: Typically, the smaller part of your monthly payment goes toward phone service and the bigger chunk is for cellular data, which is technojargon for accessing the Internet on your Droid 4. And, ho boy, you can do a lot with that Internet connection. This chapter covers some of the basic, most popular stuff.

I recommend using the Droid 4's Wi-Fi connection for extensive Internet access. Especially at 4G speeds, exceeding your monthly data plan allotment and racking up some extra fees is easy. Accessing the Internet through Wi-Fi avoids those surcharges. See Chapter 13 for more information on Wi-Fi.

The Web on Your Droid 4

Your phone comes with Browser, a web-browsing app that's similar to the one you use on a computer. Of course the Droid 4 lacks the roomy screen and full-sized keyboard found on a computer. Still, the basic web browsing experience remains the same. This section provides a quick orientation to your phone's web browsing capabilities.

Surfing the web

When you first open the Browser app, you're taken to the home screen. As shown in Figure 8-1, the standard home screen is the Google website.

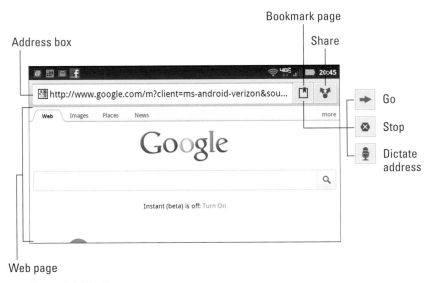

Figure 8-1: The Browser app.

To help you get the most out of viewing a web page on your Droid 4, here are a few tips and tricks:

- ✔ Pan the web page by dragging your finger across the touchscreen. You can pan up, down, left, and right.

- ✔ Double-tap the screen to zoom in or zoom out.

- ✔ Pinch the screen to zoom out, or spread two fingers to zoom in.

- ✔ Tilt the phone to its side to read a web page in landscape mode. Then you can spread or double-tap the touchscreen to make teensy text more readable.

- ✔ To visit a web page, type its address in the Address box (labeled in Figure 8-1). You can also type a search word, if you don't know the exact address of a web page.

- ✔ If you don't see the Address box, swipe your finger so that you can see the top of the window, where the Address box lurks.

- ✔ Touch a link on the screen to "click" it and visit another web page.

 ✔ You can use the arrow keys on the sliding keyboard to hop between links on a web page. Use the OK button to "click" a highlighted link.

 ✔ To stop a web page from loading, touch the stop (X) button that appears to the right of the Address box (refer to Figure 8-1).

 ✔ To reload a web page, press the Menu soft button and choose the Refresh command. Refreshing updates a website that changes often or reloads a web page that may not have completely loaded the first time.

Going back and forth

To return to a previous web page, press the Back soft button, or if the sliding keyboard is extended, press the Del (Backspace) key.

The Droid also has a Forward button in the Browser app: Press the Menu soft button and choose the Forward command.

To review the long-term history of your web browsing adventures, follow these steps:

1. **Press the Menu soft button.**

2. **Choose Bookmarks.**

3. **At the top of the Bookmarks page, choose History.**

   In the Internet app, touch the History button on the bottom right of the screen.

To view a page you visited weeks or months ago, you can choose a web page from the History list.

To clear the History list, press the Menu soft button while viewing the list and choose the Clear History command.

Working with bookmarks

Just as a desktop computer's web browser has bookmarks, the Browser app on your Droid 4 uses them as well. You can create bookmarks for your favorite websites or other web pages you want to return to later. Then you use the bookmarks to quickly visit those sites.

Here's how the whole bookmarking thing works:

1. **Visit the web page you want to bookmark.**

2. **Touch the Bookmark icon, found at the top of the Browser app screen (and labeled in Figure 8-1).**

   If you'd rather not scroll to the top of the screen, press the Menu soft button and choose the Bookmark command.

   You see the Bookmarks screen, looking similar to what's shown in Figure 8-2. The screen lists your bookmarks as website thumbnail previews.

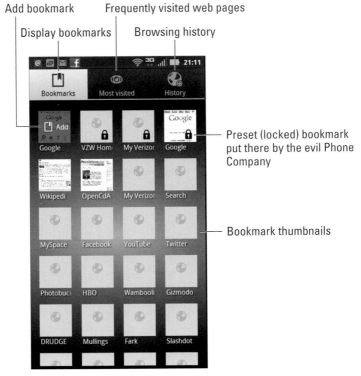

Figure 8-2: Bookmarks in the Browser app.

3. **Touch the Add button.**

   The Add button appears in the upper left square on the Bookmarks screen (refer to Figure 8-2). The button has the name of the current site or web page you're viewing just below the square.

4. **If necessary, edit the bookmark name.**

   The bookmark is given the web page name, which might be kind of long. I usually edit the name to fit below the thumbnail square.

5. **Touch OK.**

After the bookmark is set, it appears in the list of bookmarks. You can swipe the list downward to see the bookmarks and all their fun thumbnails.

✔ Alas, I know of no way to sort or rearrange the bookmarks.

✔ To visit a bookmark, press the Menu soft button and choose the Bookmarks command. Touch a bookmark thumbnail to visit that site.

✔ Remove a bookmark by long-pressing its thumbnail on the Bookmarks screen. Choose the command Delete Bookmark. Touch the OK button to confirm.

✔ When held horizontally, the Droid 4 displays its bookmark thumbnails in a long list that you can swipe left or right.

Video Fun on YouTube

One of the most popular places to visit on the web is YouTube. It's the place to go to see all sorts of videos, from historical to comical, from homemade to professional quality. You can use the Browser app to visit the YouTube website, but a better option is to the use the YouTube app that comes pre-installed on your Droid 4.

The YouTube app is found on the Apps menu. After opening it, you'll see a list of popular videos. To see your personal channel, press the Menu soft button and choose the My Channel command. If prompted, choose your Google Gmail account, and then you'll see a screen similar to what's shown in Figure 8-3.

See your subscriptions   Upload a video

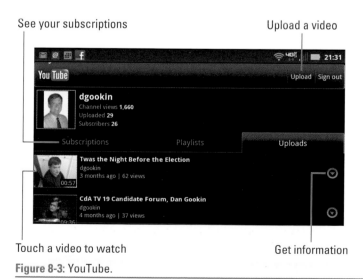

Touch a video to watch   Get information

Figure 8-3: YouTube.

To view a video, touch its name or icon in the list. You might want to press the Menu soft button and choose the Home command so that you can see popular videos beyond those channels you've subscribed to.

To search for a video, press the Search soft button while using the YouTube app. Type or dictate what you want to search for, and then peruse the results.

✔ You can touch the Upload button (refer to Figure 8-3) to shoot and then immediately send a video to YouTube. Refer to Chapter 9 for information on recording video.

✔ Not all YouTube videos can be viewed on mobile devices.

The Droid 4 Gets Social

Once upon a time, the Internet existed for e-mail. Then came the web and online everything. But recently, the focus of the Internet is the social networking phenomena. Because the Droid 4 is an Internet gizmo, you can use it to serve your social networking needs. This section shows some of what you can do.

Configuring social networking

To get things started with social networking on your Droid 4, open the Social Networking app. You'll find it dwelling on the Apps menu.

If you haven't yet added any of your social networking accounts, you'll see an Add Social Network button when you first start the Social Networking app. Touch that button and you'll be taken to the My Accounts app, where you can choose social networking sites to add.

For example, to add your Facebook account on the Droid 4, choose the Facebook icon, then type your e-mail address and Facebook password. Ditto for Twitter and whatever other social networking accounts appear on the Set Up Accounts screen.

After you've added social networking accounts, you use the Social Networking app to check what your friends are up to or to set your status. See the next section.

✔ You can also use the My Accounts app to add your social networking accounts to the Droid 4's repertoire. See Chapter 6 for additional information on the My Accounts app.

✔ If you don't yet have any social networking accounts, use a computer to set things up on the Internet. That way, you have a full screen and keyboard to help you create and configure your accounts

✔ The Droid 4 merges information about your social networking friends into its address book. New entries are created for folks not already in the address book, and if images are available for your friends already in the address book, they're automatically updated based on their social networking images.

Finding out what's going on

After getting your accounts set up, the Social Networking app takes on a new look, as shown in Figure 8-4. After starting the app, you see a list of status updates, news, and tweets from your social networking pals. Tiny icons flag the various social networking sites from which the information is pulled, as illustrated in the figure.

Services

Notification icon   Refresh feeds

```
📘📷📋                         🛜 4⬆ ▂▂ 22:38
Social Networking
⊙ All services          🔄   [ Me ▐ ]      ── See only personal items

    Jim Naiseum              5:18 PM
    Quick medical question: Lawn dart
    to the head. Remove or keep in?
                                    📘

    Ann Oying                4:53 PM
    Just joined FarmVille and now I'm
    going to bother you about it forever.
                                    📘 ── Facebook item

    Alphanso Gordo           4:53 PM
    I can see my toes!
                                    📘

    Steak & Stuff            4:46 PM
    Special today only: Week-old crab.
    We have a ton of it, and the health
    inspector is coming Monday. It has
    to go 'cause it's stinking up the place!
                                    🔲 ── Twitter item

    Elmer the Chef           4:42 PM
    Elmer the Chef has shared a link
    Embracing Your 'Good Enough' Cook - Flour
```

Figure 8-4: Social networking updates.

Touching an entry displays more details, such as comments, links, or images. For example, if you want to "like" an item in Facebook, touch that item to see the details. Touch the Like button on the details screen to like the post, or touch the Add Comment button to express your opinion.

  ✔ Updates to your social networking sites are flagged by notification icons, as illustrated in Figure 8-4. See Chapter 2 for information on reviewing notifications.

    • To see only information intended for you, touch the Me button at the top of the screen.

  ✔ Use the Services button (labeled in Figure 8-4) to choose those sites you want to view. Choose the All Services item to see updates from all your social networking sites.

Updating your status

The whole point of social networking is to be social. Although you're free to use the Social Networking app to view what others are sharing, a big part of social networking is sharing the details of your own existence. That's what makes social networking so interesting — or not.

To update your status in the Social Networking app, follow these steps:

  1. **Press the Menu soft button.**

  2. **Choose the Set Status command.**

  3. **Type your status update — a personal tidbit, a thought, or what you're doing at the moment.**

  4. **Touch the To button.**

     A list of social networking sites appears.

  5. **Select which services you'll be updating.**

     In Figure 8-5, both Facebook and Twitter are selected for updating. If you'd rather choose one or the other, select them from the To button's menu.

  5. **If you want to attach your current location or a web page link, touch the paperclip icon.**

  6. **Touch the Post button to share your status.**

     Your social networking sites are updated immediately.

Sites to post to

Post your new status

Type your status

Attach location or website link

Current Facebook status

Current Twitter tweet

Figure 8-5: Sharing your life with the universe.

When posting to Facebook, your status explains that you posted using a mobile device. This text is a clue to others that you used your phone to set your status.

✔ You can slap down various social networking widgets on the Droid 4's Home screen. These widgets can be used to monitor your social networking feeds, update your social networking status, and perform a number of other interesting things. See Chapter 15 for information on installing widgets on the Home screen.

✔ You can't un-post a status using the Social Networking app. For that kind of magic, I recommend visiting the social networking site on a computer.

Using the Facebook app

If you really like Facebook, specifically all the things Facebook lets you do on a computer, I recommend visiting the Play Store and obtaining the Facebook app. For convenience, you can scan the QR code in the margin to obtain a copy.

Unlike the Social Networking app, the Facebook app is specific to the Facebook social network. The main screen, shown in Figure 8-6, tries to emulate the Facebook experience on the computer desktop. If you're familiar with using Facebook on the web, the items on the Facebook app will be familiar.

Facebooky things to do   Notification

Comment/Like

News feeds and updates

Figure 8-6: The Facebook app.

Using the Facebook app interface, you can easily set your status, upload a picture, or check in to a location. Or just peruse the news or updates as you would on a computer. Updates, messages, and requests are accessed at the top of the screen, using icons similar to what you find on the Facebook website.

✔ Yes, you have to sign into your Facebook account on the Facebook app, even though you may have already done so in the Social Networking app. That's because the Facebook app is a separate app.

✔ Keep in mind that the Facebook app is redundant to the Social Networking app. That shouldn't be a problem, save for duplicate notification icons you'll see atop the Droid 4 touchscreen.

✔ To sign out of the Facebook app, touch the Menu soft button and choose the Logout command. Touch the Yes button to confirm. If you don't see the Logout command, press the Back soft button to get to the main Facebook screen, then try again.

Tweeting with Twitter

 Just as there is a unique Facebook app, there is also a unique Twitter app. You can use it to fulfill your tweeting desires, should you be enamored with the Twitterverse. You can obtain the official Twitter app by scanning the QR code in the margin or by visiting the Play Store to download the app.

If you're unfamiliar with Twitter, I'm happy for you. I'm not a Twitter fan, but those who are just can't seem to live without it.

You use Twitter to share your thoughts or spread news with the world, in chunks of text 140 characters or fewer. Such textual nuggets are called *tweets*, and the Twitter app helps you share and witness various tweets anywhere you go with your Droid 4.

Sharing a picture

 Although the various social networking apps have methods for taking or uploading images from your Droid 4, a better approach is to use the Share icon. Whenever you view a picture or video on your phone, you may see the Share icon, as shown in the margin. Touch that icon to see a pop-up menu of apps or methods for sharing the media. Choosing a social networking app from the menu is the best way to share that image or video.

I recommend that the image be stored on your Droid 4 or taken using the Camera app. See Chapter 9 for details on taking pictures or shooting video with your phone.

Sometimes you may find a social networking app that features a camera button. If so, you can use that button to instantly snap a picture and upload it to the social networking site. Beyond that, the best way to upload a picture is to use the Camera app to take the picture and then use a Share command to send the picture to your social universe. Here are the general steps to follow:

1. **View the image you want to share.**

   You can view the image immediately after you take it or in the My Gallery app.

 2. **Touch the Share button, found at the bottom of the screen.**

   To see the Share button, you may need to touch the screen so that the onscreen menu appears. If you still don't see a Share button, press the Menu soft button and look for a Share command.

3. **From the menu that appears, choose the Facebook or Twitter command to share the image on your social networking site.**

4. **Replace the image's long, cryptic name with a more appropriate description.**

   The name shown is the image's filename as it's stored on your phone. Long-press the name to select it, and then type something new.

5. **Touch the Send button to upload the image and its description.**

In just a few Internet seconds, the image is uploaded, online, and available for viewing by your friends, fans, and followers.

Chapter 9

Pretty as a Picture

*A*s a camera snob, I fully understand that my fancy camera takes far better pictures than the Droid 4. But I don't always carry my camera with me. I do, however, always have my phone. Therefore, most of those precious moments — birthdays, fun with friends, traffic accidents, and UFO sightings — are captured using my phone, not the much-better camera that works only as a camera. This chapter explains how you, too, can use your Droid 4 as a camera to capture life as it goes on around you.

The Droid 4 Camera

Once upon a time, having a camera wasn't enough. You also needed something called *film*. And taking a picture wasn't the final step: That film had to be *developed*. The entire picture-taking process was often a multiday, if not multiweek, ordeal.

Those days are long gone. Armed with your Droid 4, you can take and instantly view pictures anytime, anywhere.

Snapping a picture

To use your Droid 4 phone as a camera, you have to hold the phone away from your face, which I hear is hell to do when you wear bifocals. Before doing this, start the Camera app, which may be found on the Apps menu or, more conveniently, on the dock, right next to the Apps icon.

After starting the Camera app, you see the main Camera screen, as illustrated in Figure 9-1. The controls shown in the figure eventually disappear, leaving the full screen to preview the image.

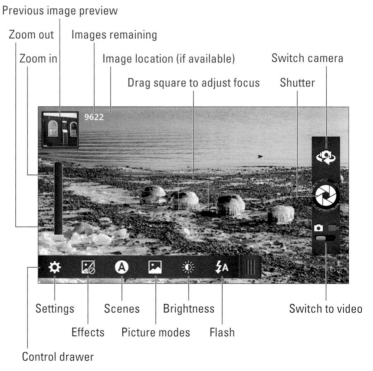

Previous image preview

Zoom out | Images remaining

Zoom in | Image location (if available) Switch camera

Drag square to adjust focus Shutter

Settings Scenes | Brightness Switch to video

Effects Picture modes Flash

Control drawer

Figure 9-1: Your phone as a camera.

To take a picture, point the camera at the subject and touch the Shutter button (labeled in Figure 9-1).

After you touch the Shutter button, the camera will focus, you may hear a mechanical shutter sound play, and the flash may go off. You're ready to take the next picture.

To preview the image you just snapped, touch previous image preview that appears in the upper-left corner of the screen (labeled in Figure 9-1).

✔ You can quickly unlock the Droid 4 into the Camera app by sliding the Camera button to the left on the main unlocking screen. See Chapter 1 for more on the unlocking screen.

✔ The camera focuses automatically, though you can drag the focus square around the touchscreen to specifically adjust the focus (refer to Figure 9-1).

✔ You can zoom in or out by using the onscreen controls or by pressing the Volume Up or Down button, respectively. Because the zoom is a *digital* zoom, the image is magnified. (In an *optical* zoom, magnification is done by adjusting the camera's lens.)

✔ If the onscreen controls disappear, touch the screen again to bring them back.

✔ Pressing the Menu soft button displays the control drawer.

✔ The phone can be used as a camera in either landscape or portrait orientation, though the phone's controls and gizmos are always presented in landscape format.

✔ You can take as many pictures with your Droid 4 as you like, as long as you don't run out of storage for them on the phone's internal storage or microSD card.

✔ If your pictures appear blurry, ensure that the camera lens on the back of the Droid 4 isn't dirty.

✔ Use the My Gallery app to preview and manage your pictures. See the later section, "A Phone Full of Photos."

✔ The Droid 4 not only takes a picture but also keeps track of where you were located on planet Earth when you took the picture. See the section "Setting the image's location" for details.

✔ The Droid 4 stores pictures in the JPEG image file format. Images are stored in the `dcim/Camera` folder; they have the `jpg` filename extension. If available, images are stored on the microSD card. You can change the storage location by pulling out the control drawer and choosing the gear icon. Choose the storage location and select either Internal Phone Storage or SD Card.

Deleting an image immediately after you take it

Sometimes, you just can't wait to delete an image. Either an agitated person is standing next to you, begging that the photo be deleted, or you are just not happy with the picture and feel the urge to smash it into digital shards. Hastily follow these steps:

1. **Touch the image preview that appears in the upper-left corner of the screen (refer to Figure 9-1).**

   After touching the preview, you see the full-screen image.

2. **Touch the More button.**

   The More button appears in the lower right corner of the image preview, shown in Figure 9-2. If you don't see the More button (or any of the buttons on the preview screen), touch the screen and they'll reappear.

Return to Camera app

Coeur d'Alene, Idaho

Feb 28, 2012

Share image | More button

Comment (social networking images only)

Figure 9-2: Previewing an image.

3. **Choose the Delete command.**

4. **Touch the OK button to confirm.**

   The image has been banished to bit hell.

 To return to the Camera app, touch the Camera button, found in the upper-left corner of the preview screen.

Setting the flash

The camera on the Droid 4 has three flash settings, as shown in Table 9-1.

Table 9-1	Droid 4 Camera Flash Settings	
Setting	*Icon*	*Description*
Auto		The flash activates during low-light situations, but not when it's bright out.
On		The flash always activates.
Off		The flash never activates, even in low-light situations.

To check the flash setting, look at the Flash button on the control drawer (refer to Figure 9-1). The button's icon confirms the current flash setting, which is Auto in the figure. Touch the Flash button to change the setting.

A good time to turn on the flash is when taking pictures of people or objects in front of something bright, such as Uncle Tony holding his bowling trophy in front of an exploding volcano.

Changing the image's resolution

You'll hear a lot of technobabble when it comes to digital photography and an image's resolution. Suffice it to say, the higher the resolution, the more detail in the image. You need that detail only when editing an image or when enlarging it for printing. Otherwise, fussing over image resolution is pointless.

On the Droid 4, image resolution is set in the Camera app: Pull out the control drawer and touch the Settings button (labeled in Figure 9-1). If a check mark appears by the Widescreen option, the resolution is set to 6MP. Remove the check mark to set the resolution to 8MP.

Press the Back soft button to dismiss the Settings menu, and then press the Menu soft button to close the control drawer.

✔ Image resolution is set *before* you snap the picture.

✔ The two image resolutions available to the Droid 4's camera have more to do with taking a widescreen shot versus a normal (non-widescreen) shot than anything else.

✔ The Droid 4's front-facing camera has a fixed resolution of 1MP.

 ✔ MP stands for *megapixel* and is a measurement of the amount of information stored in an image. One megapixel is approximately one million pixels, or individual dots that compose an image.

Taking a self-portrait

Who needs to pay all that money for a mirror when you have the Droid 4? Well, forget the mirror. Instead, think about taking all those self-shots without having to second-guess whether the camera is pointed at your face.

To take your own mug shot, start the Camera app and touch the Switch Camera button (labeled in Figure 9-1). When you see yourself on the screen, you're doing it properly.

Smile. Click. You got it.

Touch the Switch Camera button again to direct the Droid 4 to use the main camera again.

Shooting a panoramic image

A *panorama* is a wide shot, like a landscape, a beautiful vista, or a family photograph where everyone has cooties. You can take a picture as wide as you like using the Droid 4 Camera app, providing that you switch the camera into panoramic mode. Obey these steps:

1. **Start the Camera app.**

2. **Press the Menu soft button to slide out the control drawer.**

3. **Choose Panorama from the Picture Modes button's menu.**

   The Picture Modes icon was shown earlier, in Figure 9-1.

4. **Hold your arms steady.**

5. **Touch the Shutter button.**

   You see a white frame on the screen, which approximates the last shot. Arrows point in the four directions in which you can pan. The Shutter button changes to the Stop button.

6. **Pivot slightly to your right (or left or up or down, but you must continue in the same direction).**

   As you move the camera, the white frame adjusts to your new position. The Droid 4 beeps as the next image in the panorama is snapped automatically. All you need to do is keep moving.

7. **Continue pivoting as you take subsequent shots.**

8. **To finish the panorama, touch the Stop button (formerly the Shutter button).**

   After the last image is snapped, wait while the image is assembled.

The Camera app sticks the different shots together, creating a panoramic image.

The Droid 4 camera automatically captures the panoramic shot. You touch the Shutter button only when you're done.

To restore the Camera app to normal operating mode, repeat Steps 2 and 3, but choose the Single Shot mode in Step 3.

Setting the image's location

The Droid 4 not only takes a picture but also keeps track of where you're located on the globe when you take the picture — if you've turned on the Geo-Tag feature. Here's how to ensure that Geo-Tag is on:

1. **While using the Camera app, extend the control drawer.**

   You can press the Menu soft button to extend the control drawer.

2. **Touch the Settings (gear) icon.**

3. **Ensure that a green check mark appears in the Geo-Tag box.**

   If not, touch the gray box to put a check mark there.

4. **If prompted, touch the Agree button without reading the legal mumbo-jumbo in the Phone Location Settings dialog box.**

   I've consulted with an attorney, and he simply touches the Agree button without reading the text, too.

5. **Press the Back soft button to close the Settings menu, and then press the Menu soft button to withdraw the control drawer.**

Not everyone is comfortable with having the phone record a picture's location, so you can turn off the option. Just repeat these steps, but in Step 3 remove the green check mark by touching the box.

Adding effects

There is no such thing as black-and-white film when it comes to digital photography. In fact, there really is no black-and-white film, either: It's either grayscale or monochrome because, as my mother constantly reminds me, "Nothing in this world is black or white; it's all shades of gray."

My siblings and I call that her "Shades of Gray" speech. Anyway.

Although you can't change digital film, you can change camera effects in the Droid 4's Camera app: Slide out the control drawer and touch the Effects button (labeled in Figure 9-1). You'll see a pop-up palette of delightful screen effects, as shown in Figure 9-3.

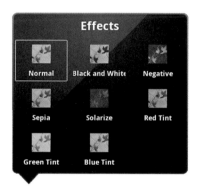

Figure 9-3: Various photographic effects.

To use an effect, pluck it from the list. The screen immediately shows the results of that effect, displaying the image in black and white (sorry, Mom), sepia, green, or whatever other effect you chose.

To return the effect back to normal, choose the Normal option.

You Ought to Be in Video

The same technology that's crammed into your Droid 4 to take still pictures can be used to record video. In fact, you use the same app on your phone — the Camera app. Sneaky, eh?

Recording video

To run the risk of an Oscar nomination, start the Camera app and flip the switch to activate video mode by touching the Switch to Camera button labeled in Figure 9-1. If you're quick, you'll see a large camcorder silhouette on the touchscreen. After that, you'll behold the Camera app in video recording mode, as shown in Figure 9-4.

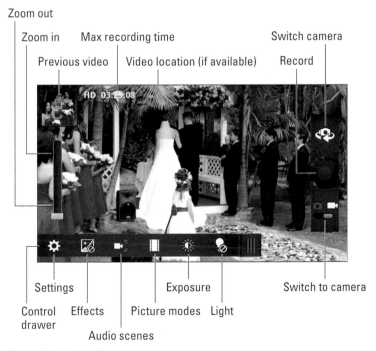

Zoom out

Zoom in   Max recording time   Switch camera

Previous video   Video location (if available)   Record

Settings   Exposure   Switch to camera

Control   Effects   Picture modes   Light
drawer
    Audio scenes

Figure 9-4: Lights! Camera! Action!

Start shooting video by pressing the Record button.

While the phone is recording, the Record button changes to the Stop button. A Mute button appears on the touchscreen, which you can touch to mute sound recording.

To stop recording, touch the Stop button.

✔ Hold the phone steady! The camera records images when you whip around the phone, but such wild gyrations render the video unwatchable.

✔ The video's duration depends on its resolution (see the next section) as well as on the storage available on your phone. The maximum recording time is shown on the screen before you shoot. While you record, elapsed time appears.

✔ In addition to the zoom controls on the screen, you can use the volume control to zoom in or out as you record video.

✔ You can use the Menu soft button to slide the control drawer in and out.

✔ Visual effects (the cheap kind, not the Hollywood CGI kind) can be applied to the video. Touch the Effects button on the control drawer to review the available visual effects.

✔ Recorded video is saved in the phone's storage — primarily, the microSD card. You can change this location by dragging out the control drawer and touching the Settings (gear) icon. Choose Storage Location, and then choose either Internal Phone Storage or SD Card.

✔ Recorded video is stored on the Droid 4 using the MPEG 4 video file format. The video files are located in the dcim/ Camera folder and have the mp4 filename extension.

Setting video quality

Although it may seem that choosing high quality or HD (high definition) all the time for videos is the best option, that's not always the case. For example, video you shoot for YouTube need not be of HD quality. Multimedia text messaging (also known as Multimedia Messaging Service, or *MMS*) video should be of very low quality or else the video doesn't attach to the message. Also, HD video occupies a heck of a lot of storage space.

To set the video quality, press the Menu soft button to pull out the control drawer and then touch the Settings (gear) icon. Choose the Video Resolution command. If you don't see Video Resolution, you need to switch the Camera app to video recording mode.

Here's a rundown of the options and my recommendations for using them:

- **HD+ (1080p):** The highest-quality setting is best suited for video you plan to show on a large-format TV or computer monitor. It's useful for video editing or for showing important events, such as Bigfoot sightings.

- **High Definition (720p):** The second-highest-quality setting, which would be a good choice if you need to record longer but still want high quality. The Droid 4 camera uses this setting automatically.

- **DVD (720 x 480):** This option has good quality for shooting video when you don't know where the video will end up.

- **VGA (640 x 480):** This setting, good for quality Internet video, doesn't enlarge well.

- **QVGA (320 x 240):** This setting is designed for use with text messaging video attachments.

Check the video quality *before* you shoot! Especially if you know where the video will end up (on the Internet, on a TV, or in an MMS message), it's best to set the quality first.

Recording a video message

You have two options to choose from for shooting video on the Droid 4: Normal Video and Video Message. The Video Message option is especially designed for quick uploading to the Internet or for adding an attachment to an e-mail or MMS (multimedia) text message.

To set the Video Message option, follow these steps in the Camera app:

1. **Switch the Camera app to video recording mode.**

2. **Press the Menu soft button to pull out the control drawer.**

3. **Touch the Picture Modes (filmstrip) icon and choose Video Message.**

4. **If you're recording yourself, touch the Switch Camera button to use the front-facing camera.**

5. **Touch the Record button to start.**

   Do something interesting.

6. **Touch the Stop button when you're done.**

The low-resolution setting in this recording mode makes the recorded message ideal for attaching to an e-mail or a text message because the message's file size is smaller.

- ✓ To attach video to a text message, start the Text Messaging app and press the Menu soft button. Choose the Insert command, and then select Existing Video. Refer to Chapter 6 for more information on text messaging.

- ✓ To add the video to an e-mail message composed in the Email app, press the Menu soft button and choose Attach Files. Choose My Gallery from the Attach Files menu, and choose your video from the Select an Item screen.

- ✓ Keep the video message short! Short is good for a video message attachment.

Shedding some light on your subject

You don't need a flash when recording video, but occasionally you need a little more light. You can manually turn on the Droid 4's LED flash to help: From the control drawer, touch the Light icon. Choose Light On to turn on the LED light on the back of the camera.

Turning on the LED light consumes a hefty portion of the phone's battery power. Use the LED light sparingly.

A Phone Full of Photos

You probably can guess that the pictures and videos you take with your Droid 4 are stored inside the phone somewhere. If you've been paying attention, you might be able to answer astutely that the images are stored either in the phone's internal storage or on the microSD card. That answer is correct but doesn't explain how to view the pictures and videos stored inside your phone. This section answers that question.

Visiting the My Gallery app

The Droid 4's picture album is found in an app called My Gallery. You can find the My Gallery app on the Apps menu, just like every other dangdoodle app on your phone.

The My Gallery app's main screen is shown in Figure 9-5. The center of the screen shows social networking images, which appear if you've added social networking accounts to your phone (see Chapter 11). The buttons on the right let you browse other parts of your photo album, depending on the image's source or how the images are organized.

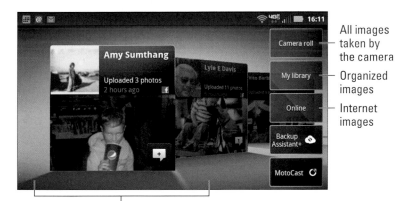

All images taken by the camera

Organized images

Internet images

Social networking image updates

Figure 9-5: The My Gallery app.

To see pictures you've taken with the Droid 4's camera, touch the Camera Roll button. You'll see a slate of thumbnail images, stacked in chronological order. Touch an image to view it full-screen. Or when you touch a video you've recorded with the phone, you can play the video full-screen.

The My Library button displays images organized into albums. The Droid 4 automatically creates albums separating still images from videos. You can choose the Folders item from the menu shown in Figure 9-6 to see images organized by source as well as by albums you've created yourself.

The Online button displays albums linked from online sources, such as Facebook, Picasa, and other online sources. To have those albums show up, you must add their online accounts to your Droid 4. The steps you follow to add an e-mail account can be used to add any online service account; see Chapter 6 for more info.

 Press the Back soft button to back out of viewing an image and return to the album. Likewise, press the Back soft button to return to the main Library screen after you're done viewing an album.

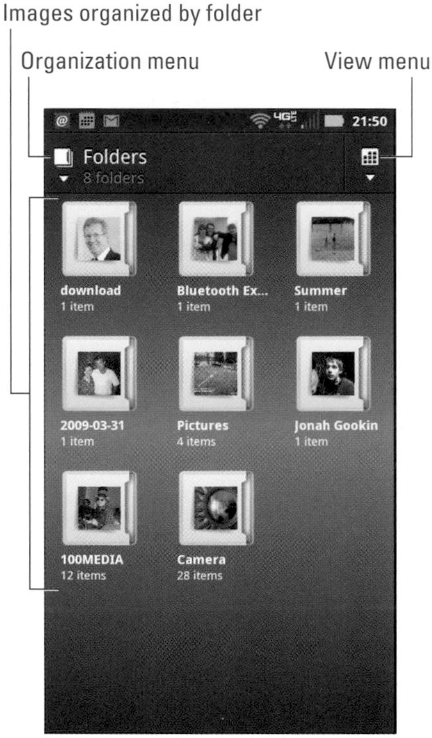

Images organized by folder

Organization menu   View menu

Figure 9-6: Organizing images by album.

Viewing an image's location on the map

When an image has been geo-tagged, you can use the My Gallery app to preview not only that image but also the location where the image was taken. Follow these steps in the My Gallery app:

1. **Touch the image so that you can view it full-screen.**

2. **Touch the More button.**

   The button is in the lower right corner of the screen, as shown in Figure 9-2. If you don't see the button, touch the screen and it appears.

3. **Choose the Map command.**

   Assuming that the image was geo-tagged, and that the geo-tag was accurate, you're switched to the Maps app, where the image's location is pinpointed.

Press the Back soft button to return to the image in the My Gallery app.

See the earlier section "Setting the image's location" for information on activating the geo-tag for images you snap with your Droid 4.

Editing images

The best tool for image editing is a computer amply equipped with photo-editing software, such as Photoshop or one of its less expensive alternatives. Even so, it's possible to use the My Gallery app to perform some minor photo surgery. Heed these steps:

1. **View the image you want to mess with in the My Gallery app.**

2. **Touch the More button and choose Edit.**

   The More button is found in the lower-right corner of the screen. You can choose the Rotate or Crop commands directly from the Edit menu, but instead follow the next step.

3. **Choose the Advanced Editing command.**

   The image appears full-size on the screen with a row of editing command buttons along the bottom, as shown in Figure 9-7. If you're viewing the image with the phone held vertically, you can scroll the editing command buttons left and right (or just reorient the phone).

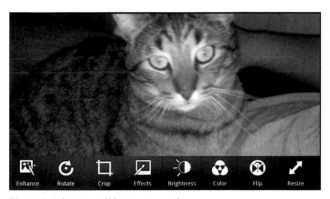

Figure 9-7: Image-editing commands.

4. **Choose a command button.**

   For example, touch the Crop button to eliminate parts of the image you don't like. Choose the Rotate command to rotate the image clockwise or counterclockwise. The remaining commands do other interesting things with the image as their names imply.

5. **Lock in a change by touching the Apply button, or dismiss your edits by touching Cancel.**

6. **Choose another editing command button, if you desire, for continued image editing.**

7. **When you're done, press the Back soft button.**

8. **Save the image if you're happy, or touch Cancel to discard any changes.**

   Touch the Yes button to lock in your changes; touch Cancel to continue editing; touch No to discard any changes you've made.

You can't edit every image, specifically images synchronized from web albums and social networking sites.

Deleting an image or a video

To prune media you no longer want in the My Gallery, summon it on the screen by itself. Touch the More button and choose the Delete command. Touch the OK button to delete the image. It's gone.

You can delete an image also by long-pressing its thumbnail and choosing the Delete command from the Picture Options menu. Touch the OK button to confirm.

✔ You cannot undelete an image after you've removed it from the phone, so exercise caution when deleting.

✔ You can't delete some images on your Droid 4, specifically images brought in from social networking sites or from online photo-sharing albums.

Sharing your images

Images don't need to be bottled up inside your phone. Nope, you can take advantage of the Share command or Share button to liberate images and videos, setting them free on the Internet for others to enjoy.

A Share button is available when you view an image full-screen in the My Gallery app. Or you can long-press a thumbnail and choose the Share command from a menu. That Share command is the key to getting the image out of your Droid 4.

After you touch the Share button or choose the Share command, you'll see a menu chock-full of methods or apps you can use to share the image or video. The variety of items depends on the apps installed on your phone as well as on which accounts you've added. Here's a run-through of some popular sharing options:

- **Photo/Video Share:** These items work with social networking sites as well as with any photo-sharing sites. You must set up your account on the phone for these options to work: Refer to Chapter 8 for information on social networking.

- **Email and Gmail:** Choosing Email or Gmail for sharing sends the media file from your phone as a message attachment. Fill in the To, Subject, and Message text boxes as necessary. Touch the Send button to send the media.

- **Picasa:** The Picasa photo-sharing site is a free service you get with your Google account. Choose this option to upload a photo to your Picasa account. Type a caption, choose an online album, and then touch the Upload button.

- **Print to Retail:** The Print to Retail option beams the image to a local photo developer for printing. You just show up an hour or so later and pick up the print.

- **Bluetooth:** Use the Bluetooth option to send (upload) the image to a Bluetooth printer. The printer must be paired and ready to use, similar to using other Bluetooth devices with the phone as discussed in Chapter 13.

- **Text Messaging:** Media can be attached to a text message, which then becomes the famous MMS (Multimedia Message Service) that I write about in Chapter 11.

- **YouTube:** The YouTube sharing option appears when you choose to share a video from your phone's photo album. After choosing that option, type a title, and optionally touch the More Details button to fill in more information about the video. Touch the Upload button to publish your creation on YouTube.

Additional options may appear on the menu, depending on which apps you have on the phone or what special features have been added by the manufacturer or cellular provider. For example, if you have the Facebook app and a Twitter client, these items appear on the bottom part of the sharing menu.

- Also see Chapter 13 for information on printing pictures stored on your Droid 4.

- I highly recommend that you connect to a Wi-Fi network when uploading YouTube videos.

✔ If you're on a 4G LTE network, you may see a warning before you upload a video, reminding you about data surcharges.

✔ You'll need to set up your Picasa account before you can use the Share button to instantly upload your pictures. You get a free Picasa account with your Google account, so visit the www.picasaweb.com site to get started. You may also have to add your Picasa account to the phone's inventory of accounts. The methods work similar to adding e-mail accounts, which is covered in Chapter 6.

✔ Some images and videos are too large to send as multimedia text messages. The phone may offer to automatically resize the images in some cases, but not all.

✔ Not every cell phone has the capability to receive multimedia text messages.

Chapter 10

Your Busy Day

Someday, technology will advance to the point where humans are too reliant upon digital servants. Call it the Robotic Revolution. The robots won't be malevolent — most evil spawns from good intentions. Instead, mankind's reliance upon electronic helpers will bring us our doom. To get there quickly, surrender your freedom now and rely on your Droid 4 to help rule your busy day.

It Can Wake You Up

O the dratted alarm clock! The bane of the modern world. The modern alarm clock is a digital creature that's annoying to set to the correct time. It's even more annoying to set the alarm time, especially with a 12-hour display. Was the alarm set for 6:00 A.M. or 6:00 P.M.? Rather than fuss over such a thing, you can simply employ your Droid 4 as your personal alarm clock.

The solution affords itself in the Alarm & Timer app. You can use that app to set multiple alarms that sound at different times or different days. Figure 10-1 shows a smattering of alarms on my Droid 4.

Touch clock to choose a new face   Alarm set

Alarm set

Alarm created but not set

Available alarms

Figure 10-1: A typical clock app.

To create an alarm in the Alarm & Timer app, follow these steps:

1. **Press the Menu soft button.**

2. **Choose Add Alarm.**

3. **Touch the Turn On Alarm item to place a green check mark in the box, activating the alarm.**

4. **Touch the item Alarm Name and give the alarm a name.**

   Alarm names will appear below the alarm on the screen, such as the text *Wake up!* below the 6:56 alarm shown in Figure 10-1.

5. **Touch the Time item and set the time when the alarm sounds.**

6. **Mess with the Sound and Vibrate options to set how the alarm annoys you.**

7. **Choose the Repeat item to set whether the alarm goes off on a schedule or is a one-time alarm.**

   Without setting a repeat time, shown as Never on the screen, an alarm sounds only once at the given time. By choosing the Repeat item you can have the alarm go off on specific days or every day.

8. **Touch the Done button to create and set the alarm.**

When the alarm triggers, the alarm's name (Step 4) appears on the touchscreen. You can swipe the screen to dismiss the alarm, or touch the phone's Volume button, which also dismisses the alarm.

Alarms must be set or else they will not trigger. To set an alarm, touch the gray box by the alarm to place a green check mark in the box. When the alarm is set, an Alarm notification icon might appear in the status area atop the touchscreen. That icon is your clue that an alarm is set and ready to trigger.

✔ When an alarm is set, the Droid 4 displays a special icon in the status bar. (The icon is also shown in the margin.)

✔ Turning off an alarm doesn't delete the alarm.

✔ To edit an alarm, touch its name.

✔ To delete an alarm, long-press it from the list and choose the Delete Alarm command. Touch the OK button to confirm.

✔ The alarm doesn't work when you turn off the phone. The alarm does go off, however, when the phone is sleeping.

✔ I charge my phone by plugging it in right on my nightstand. I put it in the optional multimedia dock, so it's propped up just like a traditional digital alarm clock. When the Droid 4 is in the multimedia dock, it displays a menu from which you can choose a Nightstand option. That option displays the current time in low intensity on the touchscreen.

✔ So tell me: Do alarms go *off* or do they go *on*?

It Can Do Your Math

Why bother using your brain when your phone has a Calculator app? You simply need to plug in the numbers — no addition, subtraction, or other mental anguish is necessary.

Summon the Calculator app from the Apps menu screen. Figure 10-2 shows the Calculator app's main screen. Also available is a second screen, chock-full of advanced and confusing mathematical functions. You can see that screen by swiping to the left. Try to remain calm when you see the second screen.

✔ Long-press the calculator's text (or results) to cut or copy the results.

✔ To clear the input all at once, long-press the Clear button.

TIP

✔ You can delete calculator input also by using the Del key on the sliding keyboard.

✔ I use the Calculator most often to determine my tip at a restaurant. In Figure 10-2, a calculation is being made for an 18 percent tip on a tab of $22.80.

22.80×.18   CLEAR

7	8	9	(	)	×
4	5	6	.	÷	−
1	2	3	0	=	+

Figure 10-2: The Calculator.

It Can Keep Your Schedule

The death knell for humanity is when the robots take control of our schedules. The automatons will tell us where to go, when to leave, where to go next, maybe even what to wear. The Droid 4 probably can't tell you what to wear (yet), but it can help you plan your day and keep up with your schedule — thanks to the Calendar app and the Google Calendar service.

Understanding the Calendar

As a Google phone, your Droid 4 takes advantage of the Google Calendar service on the Internet. The Calendar is part of your Google account. It's free, like Gmail, but not as well known. If you're not familiar with Google Calendar, I highly recommend you get started and prepare yourself to have the Droid 4 make your schedule keeping a heck of a lot easier.

Start by visiting the Google Calendar page on the Internet, at `http://calendar.google.com`. If necessary, log in using your Google account. You can use Google Calendar to keep track of dates or meetings or whatever else occupies your time. More conveniently, your Droid 4 keeps a copy of that record, allowing you to keep your schedule with you wherever you go.

- I recommend that you use the Calendar app on your phone to access Google Calendar. This method of accessing your schedule on the phone is better than using the Browser app to get to Google Calendar on the web.
- You can install the Calendar widget on the Home screen for quick access to looming appointments. See Chapter 15 for details on adding widgets to the Home screen.

Checking your schedule

To see your schedule or upcoming important events, or just to know which day of the month it is, summon the Calendar app. Like all the apps on your phone, the Calendar app is found on the Apps menu: touch the Apps icon on the Home screen to display the Apps menu, and then touch the Calendar icon to launch that app.

The Calendar app shows your schedule by month, week, or day. A fourth view, called agenda, shows your schedule as a list of appointments. In Figure 10-3, the week view is shown.

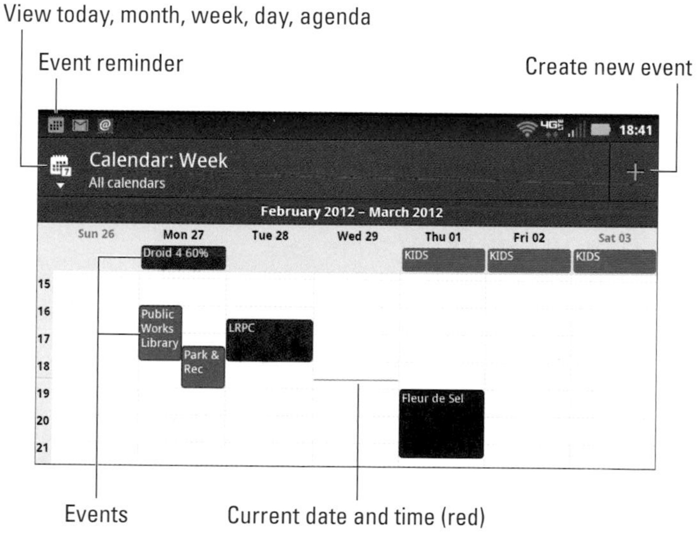

View today, month, week, day, agenda
Event reminder
Create new event
18:41
Calendar: Week
All calendars
February 2012 – March 2012
Sun 26
Mon 27
Tue 28
Wed 29
Thu 01
Fri 02
Sat 03
Droid 4 60%
KIDS
KIDS
KIDS
Public Works Library
Park & Rec
LRPC
Fleur de Sel
Events
Current date and time (red)

Figure 10-3: The Calendar's week view.

In Figure 10-3, scheduled appointments appear as colored high-lights on various days. Each color is keyed to a different calendar category. The colors help you locate events by their type or pur-pose, though using calendar categories is optional.

You can change views by using the button at the top of the screen (labeled in Figure 10-3). Figure 10-4 shows the Calendar app's month and day views.

Today   Event alarms

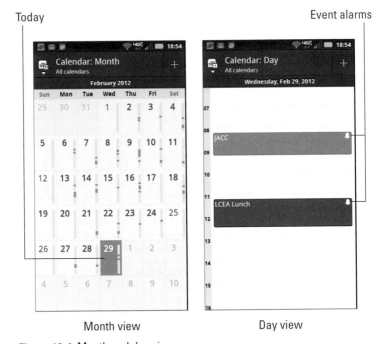

Month view   Day view

Figure 10-4: Month and day views.

✔ To quickly hop to today's date, choose the command Show Today from the View button in the upper-left corner of the Calendar app screen. Or, when there is no View button, press the Menu soft button and choose the Today command.

✔ I check week view at the start of each week to remind me of what's coming up.

✔ To control the calendar category colors in the Calendar app, press the Menu soft button and choose the Calendars command.

✔ Use your finger to flick the week and day views up or down to see your entire schedule, from midnight to midnight.

✔ Navigate the days, weeks, or months by flicking the screen with your finger. Months scroll up and down; weeks and days scroll from left to right.

✔ To go to a specific date, press the Menu soft button and choose the Go to Date command. Use the onscreen gizmo to enter a date and touch the Go button.

Reviewing events

To see all upcoming events, choose Agenda from the View button's menu. You'll see your schedule displayed as a list of events, as shown in Figure 10-5. Rather than list a traditional calendar, the Agenda screen lists only those dates with events and the events themselves.

View button menu

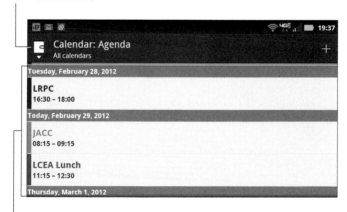

Event list

Figure 10-5: The agenda view.

To see more information about an event, touch it. Details about the event appear on the screen similar to what's shown in Figure 10-6. What you see depends on how much information you entered when the event was created. At minimum, the event has a title and time.

Time and date

Calendar category Forward event via Gmail

Event title Edit event

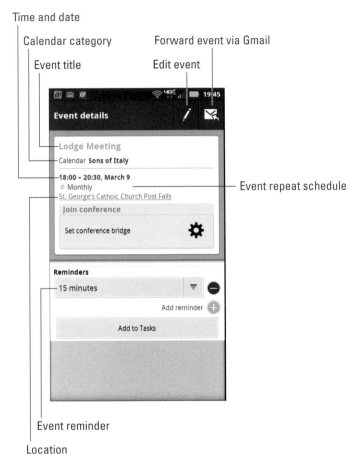

Event repeat schedule

Event reminder

Location

Figure 10-6: Event details.

 When an event location is specified, you can touch that location to view where the event takes place on the Maps app. From there, getting directions to the event's location is easy.

Creating a new event

The key to making the Calendar app work is to add events: appointments, things to do, meetings, or full-day events such as birthdays and vasectomies. To create a new event, follow these steps in the Calendar app:

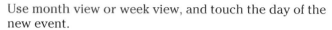

1. **Select the day for the event.**

   Use month view or week view, and touch the day of the new event.

   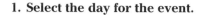

   To save time, use day view and touch the hour at which the event starts.

2. **Touch the plus sign (+) button in the upper right, or press the Menu soft button and choose the New Event command.**

   The Create Event screen appears, where you add details about the event.

3. **Choose the Calendar event.**

   Calendars are best set up on the Internet using a computer. Basically a calendar lets you organize your events by category and color. Also, you can show or hide individual calendar categories when you have a particularly busy schedule.

4. **Type the event name.**

   For example, type **Colonoscopy**.

5. **Set the event's start and end times.**

   Use the control gizmo on the screen to specify times. Or when an event is scheduled to last all day, like when your mother-in-law comes to visit for an hour, touch the All Day button to put a check mark there.

   At this point, you've entered the minimum amount of information for creating an event. Any details you add are okay but not necessary.

6. **Fill in other fields to further describe the event.**

   For example, you can touch the Where field to enter a location. The location can be used by the Maps app to help you get to your appointment. My theory is that you should specify a location as if you're typing something to search for on the map.

   A good item to set is the event reminder. That way, the phone signals you of an impending date or appointment.

7. **Touch the Save button to create the new event.**

You can change an event at any time. Simply touch the Edit Event (pencil) button in the upper right (shown in Figure 10-6) when viewing the event.

To remove an event, long-press it in the week or day view. Choose the Delete Event command. Touch the OK button to confirm.

- ✔ It's possible to create repeating events, such as anniversaries, birthdays, and weekly or monthly meetings. Use the Repetition or Repeat button to create ongoing, scheduled events.

 ✔ When you've set a reminder for an event, the phone alerts you. At minimum, you may see a Calendar Reminder notification, similar to what's shown in the margin. The phone can also be set to vibrate or sound a ringtone for impending appointments.

- ✔ To deal with an event notification, pull down the notifications and choose the event. You can touch the Dismiss button to remove event alerts.

- ✔ Alerts for events are set by pressing the Menu soft button in the Calendar app and choosing the Settings command. Use the Select Ringtone option to choose an audio alert. Use the Vibrate option to control whether the phone vibrates to alert you of an impending event.

Chapter 11

Your Leisure Activities

. . . .

In This Chapter

▶ Perusing the music library

▶ Listening to a song

▶ Copying music from your computer

▶ Purchasing music at the Play Store

▶ Using your phone as a radio

▶ Reading e-books

▶ Watching and renting videos

▶ Playing games

. . . .

*T*he theory goes that the more electronic gizmos automate human existence, the more leisure time people will have. Not so. It turns out that electronic gizmos have merely presented more options with which to occupy your leisure moments. Care to enjoy music? Your Droid 4 can help you do that. Care to read a book? Whip out the Droid 4 for that, too. You can even watch movies and TV shows on your phone. What other devices do you need in your life?

Music to Soothe the Savage Droid 4

Go ahead and toss out that portable music player gizmo, that MP3 player, that thing that rhymes with "pie rod." Your Droid 4 is more than capable of providing your digital music entertainment, thanks to the Play Music app, which is covered in this section.

Not covered in this section is the My Music app, which is provided by Verizon. Both apps are similar and do comparable things, but I favor the Play Music app.

Exploring your music library

To begin enjoying your Droid 4 as a music gizmo, you need to run the Play Music app. The app is found on the Apps menu, and you might want to consider placing that icon on your Home screen for more convenient access in the future. (See Chapter 15 for information on putting apps on the Home screen.)

The Play Music app's main screen is shown in Figure 11-1. As you can see, the screen's presentation depends on how the phone is oriented.

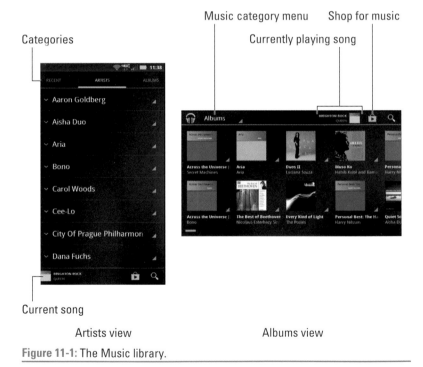

Categories

Music category menu   Shop for music

Currently playing song

Current song

Artists view   Albums view

Figure 11-1: The Music library.

The Play Music app organizes the music stored on your Droid 4 by category, as shown in Figure 11-1. The categories scroll atop the screen when the Play Music app is viewed vertically; in the horizontal orientation, the categories appear on a menu.

Here are the Play Music app's categories:

- ✔ **Recent:** Songs are listed in the order they've been recently played, with the most recently played tune appearing atop the list.

- ✔ **Albums:** Songs are organized by album. Choose an album to list its songs.

- ✔ **Artists:** Songs are listed by recording artist or group. Choose this category, and then choose an artist to see albums by that artist. Choosing an album displays the songs for that album. Some artists may have only one song, not in any particular album.

- ✔ **Songs:** All songs are listed alphabetically.

- ✔ **Playlists:** Only songs you've organized into playlists are listed by their playlist names. Choose a playlist name to view songs organized in that playlist. Using and organizing playlists is covered in my book *Android Phones For Dummies* (Wiley).

- ✔ **Genres:** Tunes are organized by their themes, such as classical, rock, or annoying.

The categories are merely ways of organizing your music, which helps you find things when you may know a song title but not the artist or album name.

- ✔ Your Droid 4 most likely didn't come with pre-installed music. If so, it was probably put there as a bonus by the place where you bought your phone. Later sections in this chapter show you how to get music for the Droid 4, either by purchasing it at the Play Store or by copying music from your computer.

- ✔ The size of the phone's storage limits the total amount of music you can keep on your phone. Also, consider that pictures and videos stored on your phone horn in on some of the space that can be used for music.

- ✔ The Play Music app assigns generic album artwork for albums that don't have their original art. The original art most often appears for music you purchase at the Play Store, though some music you import from your computer may also come with album artwork.

- ✔ I don't know of any way to add album artwork for the Play Music app.

✔ When the Droid 4 doesn't recognize an artist, it uses the title *Unknown Artist.* That situation happens most often with music (or audio files) you copy manually to the phone. Music that you purchase, or import or synchronize with a computer, generally retains the artist and album information. (Well, the information is retained as long as it was supplied on the original source.)

Listening to music

To enjoy some tunes on your Droid 4, fire up the Play Music app and choose a song from the library. You can browse by any of the categories (covered in the preceding section). To play a tune, just touch its title.

The Play Music app's player is shown in Figure 11-2. Controls on the screen let you pause, play, shuffle, and so on. Use the Show/Hide Details button to add any buttons or options which are visible in Figure 11-2 but may be hidden on your phone's touchscreen.

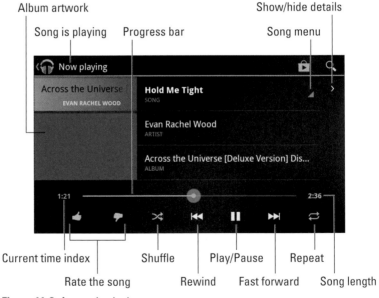

Figure 11-2: A song is playing.

While the song is playing, you're free to do anything else with the phone. In fact, the song continues to play even if the phone goes to sleep.

After the song is done playing, the next song in the list plays. The next song doesn't play if you have activated the Shuffle button (labeled in Figure 11-2). In that case, the Play Music app randomizes the songs in the list, so who knows which one will play next?

The next song also might not play if you have turned on the Repeat option. The three repeat settings — as well as the two shuffle settings — are listed in Table 11-1. To change settings, simply touch the Shuffle or Repeat button.

Table 11-1		Shuffle and Repeat Button Icons
Icon	*Setting*	*What Happens When You Touch the Icon*
	Shuffle Is off	Songs play one after the other
	Shuffle Is on	Songs are played in random order
	Repeat Is off	Songs don't repeat
	Repeat all songs	All songs in the list play over and over
	Repeat current song	The same song plays over and over

To stop a song from playing, touch the Pause button (labeled in Figure 11-2).

 When music plays on the phone, a notification icon appears, similar to what's shown in the margin. Use this notification to quickly summon the Play Music app to see which song is playing or to pause the song.

✔ The volume is set by using the Volume button on the side of the phone.

✔ Determining which song plays next depends on how you chose the song that's playing. If you choose a song by artist, all songs from that artist play, one after the other. When you choose a song by album, that album plays. Choosing a song from the entire song list causes all songs in the phone to play, one at a time of course.

✔ After the last song in the list plays, the phone stops playing songs — unless you've turned on a Repeat option, in which case the song or list plays again.

Getting music from your computer

You probably have some music on your computer, CDs you've copied or other audio that you've collected over the years. Copying that music from your computer to the Droid 4 is possible, though not entirely easy.

To copy the music from your computer to the Droid 4, you'll need to run some sort of music jukebox program on your PC. Because all Windows computers come with the Windows Media Player, the following steps are specific to that program:

1. **Connect your Droid 4 to the PC.**

   Use the USB cable that came with the phone. Attach one end to the computer and the other end to the phone.

2. **On your phone, pull down the USB Connection notification.**

3. **Choose the item Windows Media Sync.**

4. **Touch the OK button.**

   By choosing the Windows Media Sync option, you're identifying the Droid 4 as a portable media player. Windows will recognize the phone as such, which allows for easy synchronization of music, as well as pictures and video.

   On a Windows 7 computer, you may see a window open, displaying information about the Droid 4 and some media features, as shown in Figure 11-3. If you don't see the window, look for its icon on the taskbar.

5. **On your PC, start Windows Media Player.**

   On a Windows 7 computer, double-click the Manage Media on Your Device item (refer to Figure 11-3). Otherwise, you can start the Windows Media Player from the Start menu.

   You can use another media or jukebox program on your PC, if you prefer. However, the remaining steps in this section are specific to Windows Media Player.

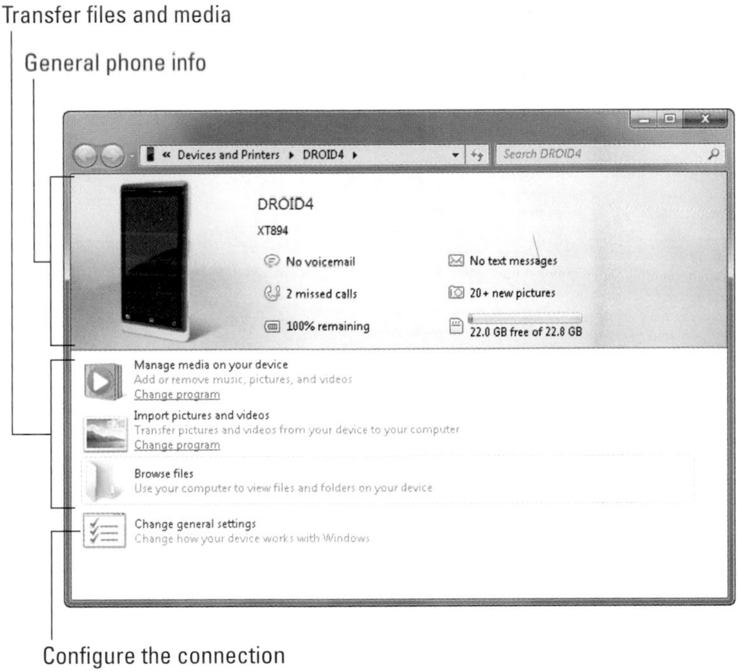

Transfer files and media

General phone info

Configure the connection

Figure 11-3: Windows 7 connects with the Droid 4.

6. **If necessary, click the Sync tab in Windows Media Player.**

   Figure 11-4 shows a Droid 4 in the Sync list on the right side of Windows Media Player. You should see something similar on your PC's screen, though you may not have the same version of Windows Media Player.

7. **Drag to the Sync area the music you want to transfer to your phone (refer to Figure 11-4).**

8. **Click the Start Sync button to transfer the music.**

9. **Close the Windows Media Player when the transfer is completed.**

10. **On the Droid 4, pull down the USB Connection notification.**

11. **Choose Charge Only to unmount the Droid 4 from the PC.**

12. **Touch the OK button to confirm.**

13. **Unplug the phone from the computer.**

Droid 4

Click to sync   Sync tab

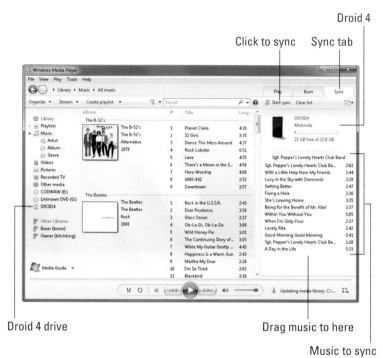

Droid 4 drive   Drag music to here

Music to sync

Figure 11-4: Windows Media Player meets Droid 4.

If you have a Macintosh or detest Windows Media Player, you can use the doubleTwist program to synchronize music between your phone and your computer. See my book *Android Phones For Dummies* (Wiley) for more information about doubleTwist.

- Your phone has room for only so much music! Don't be over-zealous when copying over your tunes. In Windows Media Player, a capacity gauge shows you how much storage space is used and how much is available on your phone. Pay heed to the indicator!

- You can't access storage (music, photos, contacts) on your Droid 4 while it's mounted to a computer for music syncing. You can access this information after you unmount the phone from the computer.

- Chapter 14 offers more information on sharing information between your computer and the Droid 4.

Buying music at the Google Play Store

When you don't have any music to copy from a computer, and you're not creative enough to write your own, you need to buy it. The place to go is the Play Store, which is the same place you go to get apps for your phone (as well as books and videos).

Chapter 12 is devoted to coverage of the Play Store. For buying music at the Play Store, follow these steps:

1. **Ensure that you're using a Wi-Fi or high-speed digital network connection.**

    Activating the Droid 4's Wi-Fi is described in Chapter 13. You can use the 4G LTE connection, but be wary of running over your monthly data allotment.

2. **Open the Play Store app.**

    You can find the app on the Apps menu.

3. **Choose the Music category from the Play Store app's main page.**

    You can visit the Music store in the Play Store by touching the Play Store icon, as shown in the margin. The icon can be found on just about every screen in the Play Music app, such as the one shown in Figure 11-1.

4. **Browse or search for the music you want.**

    To browse, choose a category from the top of the screen. Scroll the contents up or down to look for something interesting. Or you can touch the Search button (or Search soft button) and type the artist, album, or song that you're looking for.

    The results are displayed by song title and artist. Also listed is the song or album's price. Yes, these things cost money.

5. **Touch a result.**

    If the result is an album, you see the contents of the album. Otherwise, you'll see the song highlighted by itself or within an album.

    Touch the Play button next to a song to hear a brief preview. Touch the song again to stop the preview.

6. **To purchase the song or album, touch the button with the amount in it.**

   Don't fret; you're not purchasing anything yet. You'll see a second screen with more details, including the credit card you have on file with Google Checkout, plus the final Accept & Buy button.

   If you don't yet have a credit card on file with Google Checkout, you can set one up: Follow the directions on the screen.

7. **Touch the Accept & Buy button.**

8. **Wait while the music downloads.**

   Well, actually, you don't have to wait: The music continues to download while you do other things on the phone.

 The Play Store app uses the App Installed icon, shown in the margin, to tell you when the song or album has finished downloading. You can choose that item to open the Play Music app and then choose the song or album from the list of purchased (or free) music. Enjoy the tunes!

- Check out the free song of the day: Every day a song is showcased in the Google Play Music store. Reminding yourself to get that free song is a great way to quickly build your Droid 4's music library.

- You can coordinate your Google music purchases with your computer on the Internet: Visit music.google.com and sign in to your Google account. The screen lists your Play Store music purchases, which you can then listen to on any computer connected to the Internet.

- Google Play e-mails you a bill for your purchase. That bill is your purchase record, so I advise you to be a good accountant and print it and then input it into your bookkeeping program or personal finance program at once!

- See Chapter 12 for more information on the Play Store app.

Listening to live music from the Internet

Your Droid 4 can listen to that free music source called Internet radio — provided you have the proper software installed. I recommend the following three apps:

✔ TuneIn Radio

✔ Pandora Radio

✔ StreamFurious

 The TuneIn Radio app gives you access to hundreds of Internet radio stations broadcasting around the world. The stations are organized by category, so you can find just about whatever you want. Many Internet radio stations are also broadcast radio stations, so odds are good you can find a local station or two.

 Pandora Radio lets you select music based on your mood and then uses your feedback to customize the tunes you listen to. The app works like the Internet site www.pandora.com. The nifty thing about Pandora is that the more you listen, the better the app gets at finding music you like.

 StreamFurious streams music from various radio stations on the Internet. Although not as customizable as Pandora, StreamFurious uses less bandwidth so you can enjoy your music without having to risk running up digital cellular surcharges.

 I highly recommend listening to Internet radio when your Droid 4 is connected to the Internet through a Wi-Fi connection. Streaming music can use a lot of your cellular data plan's data allotment.

✔ The Droid 4 ships with the MOG app, which also lets you listen to music-on-demand from the Internet. MOG lets you listen free for a trial period; the subscription service costs about $10 a month.

✔ The Slacker Radio app also comes with your Droid 4. It's free, but you have to sign up and create an account. Then they send you e-mail, which I'd prefer not to get, which is why I recommend an app such as TuneIn Radio instead.

✔ Verizon also installs bloatware on your Droid 4 that probably includes a music subscription service or some such nonsense. I wouldn't know because I see no reason to run any Verizon app.

 ✔ *Bloatware* is the term for software included with a device, such as a computer or a smartphone. You don't have to use the software, and it generally does nothing to enhance your experience. Bloatware is like the sampling menu at a farmer's market but minus the nutritional value. The word is a combination of *bloat* and *software*.

Something to Read

An *e-book* is an electronic version of the thing you're holding in your hands right now — a book (especially if you're reading the e-book version of this book). In an e-book, the words, formatting, figures, pictures — all that stuff is simply stored digitally so that you can read it on something called an e-book reader.

The Droid 4 comes with two e-book reading apps: Google Books, which is tied into the Play Store, and the Amazon Kindle app, which taps into Amazon's vast Kindle e-book library. Both apps are covered in this section.

   ✔ The advantage of an e-book reader is that you can carry an entire library of books with you without developing back problems.

   ✔ Rather than buy a new book at the airport, consider getting an e-book instead.

   ✔ Lots of e-books are free, such as quite a few classics — including some that aren't that boring. Current and popular titles cost money, though the cost is often cheaper than the book's real-world equivalent.

   ✔ Magazine and newspaper subscriptions are also available for e-book readers.

   ✔ Not every title is available as an e-book.

Reading Google Play Books

The Play Books app allows you to read e-books purchased at the Google Play Store. The app organizes the books into a library, and displays titles for reading on your phone. The reading experience happens like this:

   1. Open the Play Books app.

   If you're prompted to turn on synchronization, touch the Turn On Sync button.

   You see your e-book library, which lists any titles you've obtained for your Google Play Books account. Or, when you're returning to the Play Books app after a break, you see the current page of the e-book you were last reading.

2. **Touch a book to open it.**

3. **Start reading.**

   Use Figure 11-5 as your guide for reading a Google Play Books e-book. Basically you just swipe the pages left to right.

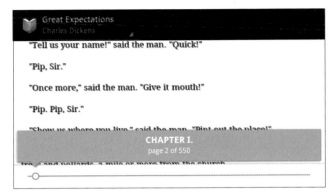

Figure 11-5: Reading an e-book in the Play Books app.

See Chapter 12 for information on purchasing books at the Google Play Store.

Synchronization allows you to keep copies of your Google Play Books e-books on all your Android devices, as well as on the `http://books.google.com` website.

Using the Amazon Kindle app

The Amazon Kindle may be the most popular e-book reader in the world. I think the folks at Amazon realize that. They also understand that you're probably not going to buy a Kindle when you already have a portable electronic gizmo such as the Droid 4. And why should you carry another gizmo, when you can use the Amazon Kindle app on your phone to read those very same e-books?

Upon starting the Amazon Kindle app, you see the Registration screen. Log in using your e-mail address and Amazon password. (The process is just like logging into the Amazon website.)

If you already have an Amazon Kindle account, your phone synchronizes with your existing Kindle library after you touch the Register button.

Choose a book from the Kindle bookshelf and start reading. The e-book–reading operation on the Kindle is similar to that on the Play Books app (refer to Figure 11-5). However, on the Kindle, you can highlight text, bookmark pages, look up a word in a dictionary, and do other keen stuff that Google will no doubt add to a future update of their Play Books app.

🖙 You purchase e-books for the Kindle app at the Kindle store using your existing Amazon account. In the Kindle app, press the Menu soft button and choose Kindle Store.

🖙 Yes, you need an Amazon account to purchase e-books (or even download freebies), so I highly recommend that you visit Amazon to set up an account if you don't already have one.

 🖙 To ensure that you get your entire Kindle library on your phone, turn on the Droid 4's Wi-Fi connection (see Chapter 13). After Wi-Fi is connected, return to the Amazon Kindle app, press the Menu soft button, and choose the Archived Items command. (Using Wi-Fi avoids data surcharges.)

Videos to View

The Google Play Store also rents videos. You can watch everything from major Hollywood releases to a few TV shows and series. The videos you rent are then viewed using the Play Videos app, found on the Droid 4's Apps menu.

Here are the general steps you take to rent and view a video on your phone:

1. **Open the Play Store app on your phone.**

2. **Choose the Movies category.**

   All movies are rentals.

3. **Browse or search for a movie.**

4. **Touch the movie's Rent button, which also lists the rental price.**

   You're not charged for touching the Rent button. Instead, you see more details, such as the rental terms. Typically, you have 30 days to watch the film. After you start watching, you can pause and resume — or watch the movie over and over — during a single 24-hour period.

5. **Choose a payment method.**

   If you don't yet have an account set up at Google Checkout, you can configure one by touching the Add Payment Method button. Otherwise, choose your Google Checkout credit card as shown on the screen.

6. **Touch the Accept & Buy button to rent the movie.**

7. **Touch the Play button to view the movie.**

The move is *streamed* to your phone, which means it's sent as you watch it. Therefore, I highly recommend two things when you're ready to watch. First, plug your phone into a power source. Second, turn on the Wi-Fi network so that you don't incur any data overages.

You don't have to view the movie right away. You can wait up to 30 days. When you're ready, start the Play Videos app and choose your rental from the My Rentals list.

You can also start the Play Videos app from the App menu to review and view your rentals as well as any personal videos you've installed on your phone.

Your Droid 4 features an HDMI output jack. You can connect a special (and not cheap) HDMI cable to the phone, which connects it to an HDMI TV set or computer monitor. That way, you can view your rental on a larger screen. Gather the family and bring the popcorn. See Chapter 14 for details on making the HDMI connection.

It Plays Games

One of the best uses of a smartphone, for all its seriousness and technology, is to play games. I'm not talking about the silly arcade games (though I admit that they're fun). No, I'm talking about some serious portable gaming.

To whet your appetite, your Droid 4 was preloaded with some sample games: Let's Golf 2, shown in Figure 11-6, and Madden NFL 12 (not shown in Figure 11-6). Both are previews, not the full games, but they're something to mess around with and give you an idea of what the phone is capable of as a game machine.

Figure 11-6: A game on your phone.

The best place to look for games is the Play Store, covered in Chapter 12. Choose the Apps category, and then choose Games. Plenty of free games are available, as well as lite versions of for-pay games.

I could recommend a few hundred games here, but I'd have to justify the "research" time to my editor, and I'm just not that creative.

Chapter 12

Apps, Apps, and More Apps

. . . .

In This Chapter

▶ Using the Play Store app

▶ Searching for apps

▶ Downloading a free app

▶ Getting a paid app

▶ Reviewing apps you've downloaded

▶ Sharing an app

▶ Updating an app

▶ Managing apps

▶ Building app groups

. . . .

*W*hat your Droid 4 can do is limited only by the software installed. While the phone does come with a smattering of basic and trial apps, far many more apps are available. You'll find them at a central repository called the Google Play Store. There you can find and download apps that extend the capabilities of your Droid 4, plus you can find and download music, books, videos, games, and more. It all starts with a visit to the Play Store.

Behold the Google Play Store

Your Droid 4 shipped with about 60 apps preinstalled — a pittance. More than 500,000 apps are available at the Google Play Store. Some cost money. Most are free. All are waiting for you to try.

✔ The Google Play Store was once called the *Android Market*. You may still see it referenced that way, or as simply the *Market*. Google changed the name in early 2012, which is why some folks and lots of documentation still mention the Android Market.

✔ The Play Store is also the place to go for downloading books, videos, and music. See Chapter 11 for information.

✔ You don't even need to know what you want at the Play Store; like many a mindless ambling shopper, you can browse until the touchscreen is smudged and blurry with fingerprints.

✔ You obtain items from the Play Store by *downloading* them into your phone. That file transfer works best at top speeds, so I highly recommend that you connect to a Wi-Fi network if you plan to obtain apps, books, or movies at the Play Store. Wi-Fi not only gives you speed but also helps you avoid data surcharges. See Chapter 13 for details on connecting your phone to a Wi-Fi network.

✔ The Play Store app is frequently updated, so its look may change from what you see in this chapter. Updated information on the Play Store can be found on my website, at www. wambooli.com/help/phone.

Visiting the Play Store

Your new app experience begins by opening the Play Store app. It's found on the Apps menu, though a shortcut icon may also be on the primary Home screen.

The main screen of the Play Store app, shown in Figure 12-1, lists an overview of all the goodies you can get for your phone. Choose the Apps category to see the Apps main screen, also shown in Figure 12-1. Use the ribbon atop the screen to browse categories and highlights, such as the Top Paid apps shown in Figure 12-1.

Top Paid category

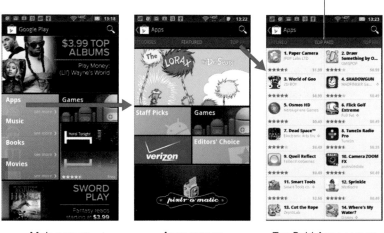

Main screen   Apps screen   Top Paid Apps screen

Figure 12-1: The Google Play Store.

As you browse, you'll eventually see a list of app tiles (refer to the rightmost screen in Figure 12-1). The app tiles give you a quick overview of the app's title, rating, and cost. Touching a tile displays more detailed information, as shown in Figure 12-2.

Rating

Video preview   Install or buy the app

Return to previous screen   Share button

Scroll down for even more

More details

Number of downloads

Figure 12-2: Details for an app.

Scroll through the app details to read its description, check out its ratings, peruse some screen shots, and look at similar or recommend apps. Key things I recommend looking for are the number of downloads and the app's rating.

When you know what you want, such as an app's name or even what it does, searching the Play Store is faster than browsing. Touch the Search button at the top of the Play Store screen (refer to Figure 12-1). Type all or part of the app's name, book, or movie title, or perhaps a description. Touch the Enter key to locate what you're looking for.

- The first time you enter the Google Play Store, you have to accept the terms of service; touch the Accept button.

- Apps you download are added to the Apps menu and become available like any other app on your phone.

- You can be assured that all apps that appear in the Play Store can be used on your Droid 4. You can't download or buy something that's incompatible with your phone.

- Pay attention to an app's ratings. Ratings are added by people who use the apps, like you and me. Having more stars is better. You can see additional information, including individual user reviews, by choosing the app.

- Another indicator of an app's success is how many times it's been downloaded. Some apps have been downloaded tens of millions of times. That's a good sign.

- In addition to getting apps, you can download widgets and wallpapers for your phone's Home screen. Just search the Play Store for *widget* or *live wallpaper.*

- See Chapter 15 for more information on widgets and live wallpapers.

Getting a free app

After you locate an app you want, the next step is to download it from the Play Store into your Droid 4. Follow these steps:

1. **If possible, activate the phone's Wi-Fi connection to avoid incurring data overages.**

   See Chapter 13 for information on connecting your phone to a Wi-Fi network.

2. **Open the Play Store app.**

3. **Locate the app you want and open its description.**

   You can browse for apps or use the Search button to find an app by name or what it does.

4. **Touch the Install button.**

   The button is found at the bottom of the app's description screen (refer to Figure 12-2). Touching the button does not immediately download or install the app.

After touching the Install button, you're shown the services that the app uses. The list isn't a warning, and it doesn't mean anything bad. The screen just confirms that the app does what it says it does, and that the Play Store is being honest with you about which resources the app uses.

5. **Touch the Accept & Download button to begin the download.**

   The app is automatically downloaded and installed onto your phone.

6. **Touch the Open button to run the app.**

   Or, if you were doing something else while the app was downloading and installing, choose the Successfully Installed notification, as shown in the margin. The notification features the app's name, with the text *Successfully Installed* below it.

At this point, what happens next depends on the app you've downloaded. For example, you may have to agree to a license agreement. If so, touch the I Agree button. Additional setup may involve setting your location, signing in to an account, or creating a profile, for example.

Grab yourself a bar code scanner app

Many apps from the Google Play Store can be quickly accessed by scanning their bar code information. You may have seen such bar codes — called QR codes — scattered about this book's margins.

What can you scan those codes with? Why, your Droid 4, of course!

By using a bar code scanner app, you can instantly read in and translate bar codes into links to that app at the Google Play Store. Further, you can scan product bar codes and see more information, including perhaps some low prices at various merchants. Some apps even let you build shopping lists by scanning bar codes of products you may already have.

Plenty of bar code apps are out there. I use one called Barcode Scanner, which is free and easy to use. Point the Droid 4's camera at a bar code and, in a few moments, you see a link or an option for what to do next. To get an app, choose the Open Browser option, which opens the Play Store on your phone. It's cinchy.

After the initial setup is complete, or if no setup is necessary, you can start using the app.

✔ The new app's icon is placed on the Apps menu, along with all the other apps on the phone.

✔ Peruse the list of services an app uses (in Step 4) to look for anything unusual or out of line with the app's purpose. For example, an alarm clock app that uses your contact list and the text-messaging service would be a red flag, especially if it's your understanding that the app doesn't need to text message any of your contacts.

Purchasing an app

Some great free apps are available, but many of the apps you dearly want probably cost money. The apps don't cost a lot of money, especially compared to the price of computer software. In fact, stewing over whether paying 99 cents for a game is worth it seems odd.

I recommend that you download a free app first, to familiarize yourself with the process.

When you're ready to pay for an app, follow these steps:

1. **Activate the phone's Wi-Fi connection.**

2. **Open the Play Store app.**

3. **Browse or search for the app you want, and choose the app to display its description.**

   Review the app's price.

4. **Touch the price button.**

   The price button replaces the Install button for free apps, as shown in Figure 12-2. It represents the app's price. For example, if the app is $0.99, the button reads $0.99.

5. **Choose your credit card.**

   The card must be on file with Google Checkout. If you don't yet have a card on file, choose the Add Payment Method option, and then choose Add Card. Fill in the fields on the Credit Card screen to add your payment method to Google Checkout.

6. **Touch the Accept & Buy button.**

   Your payment method is authorized, and the app is downloaded and installed.

Never buy an app twice

Any apps you've already purchased in the Play Store — say, for another phone or mobile device — are available for download on your current Android phone at no charge. Simply find the app. You'll see it flagged as *Purchased* in the Play Store. Touch the Install button, and then touch Accept & Download to install the already purchased app on your Droid 4.

You can review any already purchased apps in the Play Store. Touch the Menu soft button and choose My Apps. At the bottom of the list, under the heading Not Installed, you'll find any apps you've already purchased at the Play Store. You can choose an app from that list to install it on your Droid 4.

Once installed, the app can be accessed from the App menu, just like all other apps available on your phone. Or if you're still at the app's screen in the Play Store, touch the Open button.

Eventually, you receive an e-mail message from Google Checkout, confirming your purchase. The message explains how you can get a refund for your purchase. In general, you can open the app's info screen (see the section "Controlling your apps," later in this chapter) and touch the Refund button to get your money back.

Be quick on that refund: Some apps allow you only 15 minutes to get your money back. Otherwise, the refund period could be up to 24 hours. You know when the time is up because the Refund button changes its name to Uninstall.

Also see the section "Removing apps," later in this chapter.

Manage Your Apps

The Play Store app does two important jobs. Not only is it where you obtain new apps for your Droid 4, it's also the place you return to when you want to perform app management. That task includes reviewing apps you've downloaded, updating apps, organizing apps, and removing apps you no longer want or you severely hate.

Reviewing your downloaded apps

It's difficult to look at the Apps menu and determine which apps came with your Droid 4 and which you've added over time. A better place to look is the My Apps list found in the Play Store app. Follow these steps:

1. **Start the Play Store app.**

2. **Press the Menu soft button and choose My Apps.**

3. **Scroll your downloaded apps.**

The list of downloaded apps should look similar to the one shown in Figure 12-3. At the top of the list, you'll find apps installed on your phone but in need of updating. The two types of updates are automatic and manual.

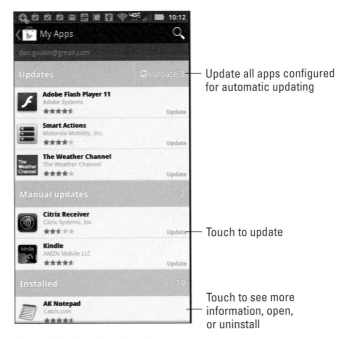

Update all apps configured for automatic updating

Touch to update

Touch to see more information, open, or uninstall

Figure 12-3: The list of installed apps.

Next in the list are categories for Installed apps and Not Installed apps. The Not Installed apps are mostly apps you've already purchased at the Play Store for other Android devices but haven't yet installed on your Droid 4.

Sharing an app

When you love an app so much that you just can't contain your glee, feel free to share it with your friends. You can easily share a link to the app in the Play Store by obeying these steps:

1. **Visit the app on your My Apps list.**

   Refer to the preceding section. Note that the app doesn't have to be on your list of apps; it can be any app in the Play Store. You just need to be viewing the app's description screen.

2. **Touch the Share button.**

   A menu appears listing various apps and methods for sharing the app's Play Store link with your pals.

3. **Choose a sharing method**

   For example, choose Text Messaging to send a link to the app in a text message.

4. **Use the chosen app to send the link.**

   What you need to do next depends on which sharing method you've chosen.

The result of these steps is that your friends receive a link. They can touch the link on their phone, or other Android device, and be whisked instantly to the Play Store, where they can view the app and easily install it on their gizmo.

Updating an app

It's the Play Store app's duty not only to get you new apps and manage your apps but also to inform you of app updates. When a new version of an app is available, you see it flagged for updating, as shown in Figure 12-3. Updating the app to get the latest version is cinchy.

From the My Apps list (refer to Figure 12-3), touch the Update button to update all the apps for which automatic updating is allowed.

Some apps must be updated individually; these are shown in the Manual Updates part of the My Apps list. To update those apps, first touch the green Update button found to the right of the app's name (refer to Figure 12-3). Then touch the Update button on the app's information screen and choose Accept & Download.

To make updating easier, open an app's information screen and place a green check mark by the item Allow Automatic Updating.

✓ The updating process often involves downloading and installing a new version of the app. That's perfectly fine; the update process does not change your settings and any app information already stored on your phone (data files, high scores, and so on).

✓ Updates to apps might be indicated also by the Updates Available notification icon, shown in the margin. Choose the Updates Available notification to be taken to the My Apps screen, where you can update your apps as described in this section.

Removing apps

You're free to kill off any app you've downloaded from the Play Store. To do so, heed these steps:

1. **Start the Play Store app.**

2. **Press the Menu soft button and choose My Apps.**

3. **Touch the app that offends you.**

4. **Touch the Uninstall button.**

   If you don't see an Uninstall button, the app is a prepackaged app included on your phone and can't be removed.

5. **Touch the OK button to confirm.**

   The app is removed.

The app continues to appear on the My Apps (downloads) list even after you've removed it. After all, you downloaded it once. That doesn't mean that the app is installed.

✓ In most cases, if you uninstall a paid app right away, your credit card or account is fully refunded. The definition of "right away" depends on the app and is stated on the app's description screen. The refund period could be anywhere from 15 minutes to 24 hours.

✓ You can always reinstall paid apps that you've uninstalled. You aren't charged twice for doing so.

✓ A handful of apps can't be removed from your phone. These include some of the basic Android apps (such as the Phone and Contacts apps) and some apps preinstalled by your cellular provider. Only if you hack into your phone through a process called *rooting* can you remove those apps. I don't recommend it.

Controlling your apps

Your Droid 4 features a secret, technical place where you can review and manage all installed apps. To visit that place, follow these steps:

1. **At the Home screen, press the Menu soft button.**
2. **Choose Settings, and then choose Applications.**
3. **Choose Manage Applications.**
4. **Choose the All tab from the top of the screen.**

   A complete list of all apps installed on your phone is displayed. Unlike the My Apps list in the Play Store app, only installed apps appear in the All tab's list.

5. **Touch an application name.**

   An app info screen appears, showing lots of trivia about the app.

Among the trivia on the application's info screen, you'll find some useful buttons. Among them, these are my favorites:

- **Force Stop:** Touch this button to halt a program that's run amok. For example, I had to stop an older Android app that continually made noise and offered no option to exit.

- **Uninstall:** Touch the Uninstall button to remove the app, which is another way to accomplish the same steps described in the preceding section.

- **Refund:** Freshly purchased apps feature a Refund button instead of an Uninstall button. Touch the Refund button to both uninstall the paid app and get your money back — but you have to be quick. After a given amount of time — anywhere between 15 minutes and 24 hours — the Refund button transforms back to the Uninstall button.

- **Move to Media Area:** Touch this button to transfer the app from the phone's internal storage to the microSD card. Doing so can free capacity on the phone's internal storage.

- **Move to Phone:** Touch this button to transfer an app from the microSD card to the phone's internal storage. (This button replaces the Move to Media Area button when an app is already dwelling on the microSD card.)

- **Share:** Touch the Share button to send a text or e-mail message to a friend. See the earlier section "Sharing an app."

Controversy is brewing in the Android community about whether to store apps on the phone's internal storage or the microSD card. I prefer the internal storage because the app stays with the phone and is always available. Further, apps stored internally won't have their shortcuts disappear from the Home screen when you access the media card from your computer.

App Groups for the Apps Menu

One thing the Play Store app doesn't do for you is organize your apps. You can ignore organization, but as the number of apps you have grows, so too will the need to keep your sanity. At that point, organization becomes a psychological necessary.

All the apps on your Droid 4 are kept on the Apps menu. You can slap a few of the apps down on the Home screen panels as short-cut icons, a task covered in Chapter 15. Or you can organize your apps into groups on the Apps Menu. Heed these steps:

1. **Touch the Apps button on the Home screen to display the Apps menu.**

2. **Touch the Groups button.**

   The Groups button is in the upper-left corner of the screen, as shown in Figure 12-4.

3. **Choose New Group.**

   You see a new screen, where you can describe the group, as shown in Figure 12-5.

4. **Name the group.**

   For example, I named by group *Games.*

5. **Choose an appropriate icon from the icons menu (to the left of the group name text field).**

6. **Touch the Save icon.**

   The Select Apps menu appears. It lists all the apps installed on your phone.

7. **Scroll through the list of apps, placing a green check mark by the apps you want to add to your group.**

   The apps are not moved; only a copy of the app (a shortcut or alias) is placed into your new group.

8. **Touch the OK button when you're done adding apps.**

   The group is created and filled with apps.

Create new group

Groups button

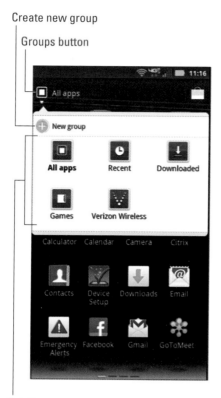

Existing groups

Figure 12-4: Apps menu groups.

Choose a group icon   Save

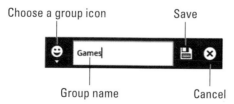

Group name   Cancel

Figure 12-5: Creating a new app group.

You can redisplay all the phone's apps by choosing the All Apps command from the Groups menu. Or you can choose any other group from the Groups menu, or create even more groups to further organize your apps.

You can edit or remove the group by long-pressing it on the Groups menu. You can even add the group to the Home screen as a shortcut, which is yet another way to organize your apps.

Chapter 13

Wireless Networking Wizardry

For any device to be truly mobile, it must not have wires. That makes sense. Well, and the device needs to be lightweight, though I suppose an elephant is mobile and lacks wires, but that's not my point. My point is that your Droid 4 offers several methods by which it dispenses with the use of wires. The topic is wireless networking, wireless communications with other gizmos, and even wireless printing.

It's a Wireless Life

Your head would doubtless explode if your eyes could see the rampant wireless communications going on all around you. Those wireless signals come from all over — even from satellites orbiting the earth. They let you talk, but most importantly, they let you communicate with the Internet. This section explains how all that's done on the Droid 4.

Understanding the digital network

Of the many fees and charges you pay on your monthly cell phone bill, the largest one is probably for the cellular data network. That network is not the wireless service you talk on (which is a much smaller charge) but is important because your Droid 4 uses the cellular data network to talk with the Internet.

Several types of cellular data network are available. The names depend on the technology used to communicate, and the type of network is chosen by your cellular provider. I shan't bore you with those details.

More important (and obvious) than the type of cellular data network is the speed at which your phone communicates with that network. The speed value appears atop the Droid 4 touchscreen in the phone status area. Here are some speed values:

- **4G LTE:** The fourth generation of digital cellular network is comparable in speed to standard Wi-Fi Internet access. 4G LTE is fast. It also allows for both data and voice transmission at the same time.

- **3G:** The third generation of wide-area data networks isn't quite as fast as 4G but is moderately tolerable for surfing the web, watching YouTube videos, and downloading information from the Internet.

- **1X:** The slowest data connection comes in several technical flavors. All 1X connections represent the same thing: the original, slow data network.

The Droid 4 always uses the fastest network available. When a 4G LTE signal abounds, the phone uses it. Otherwise, the 3G data network is chosen, followed by 1X. Or, when no cellular data network is available, that part of the status bar is blank.

- You can still make phone calls when a data network isn't available. As long as the signal strength bars on the phone's status bar show a signal present, you can receive and make phone calls.

- Accessing the digital cellular network isn't free. You've likely signed up for some form of subscription plan for a certain quantity of data when you first received your Android phone. When you exceed that quantity, the costs can become prohibitive.

- The data subscription is based on the *quantity* of data you send and receive. At 4G LTE speeds, the prepaid threshold can be crossed quickly.

Activating Wi-Fi

Wi-Fi is the same wireless networking standard used by computers for communicating with each other and the Internet. Making Wi-Fi work on your Droid 4 requires two steps. First, you must activate Wi-Fi by turning on the phone's wireless radio. The second step is connecting to a specific wireless network.

Follow these steps to activate Wi-Fi on your Droid 4:

1. **At the Home screen, press the Menu soft button.**
2. **Choose Settings, and then choose Wireless & Networks.**
3. **Choose Wi-Fi to place a green check mark by that option.**

   A green check mark indicates that the phone's Wi-Fi radio is now activated.

Next you need to connect the phone to a Wi-Fi network, which is covered in the next section.

To turn off Wi-Fi, repeat the steps in this section but in Step 3 remove the green check mark. Doing so turns off the phone's Wi-Fi access, disconnecting you from any networks.

✔ For fast Wi-Fi on/off action, you can add the Toggle: Wi-Fi widget to the Droid 4's Home screen. See Chapter 15 for infor-mation about adding widgets to the Home screen.

✔ The Wi-Fi radio places a negligible drain on the battery. If you want to save a modicum of juice, especially if you're out and about and don't plan to be near a Wi-Fi access point for any length of time, turn off the Wi-Fi radio.

✔ Using Wi-Fi to connect to the Internet doesn't incur data usage charges.

Accessing a Wi-Fi network

After activating the Droid 4's Wi-Fi radio, you can connect to an available wireless network. Heed these steps:

1. **Press the Menu soft button while viewing the Home screen.**
2. **Choose Settings, and then choose Wireless & Networks.**

3. Choose Wi-Fi Settings.

You see a list of Wi-Fi networks; in Figure 13-1, only one Wi-Fi network is available. When no wireless network is displayed, you're sort of out of luck regarding Wi-Fi access from your current location.

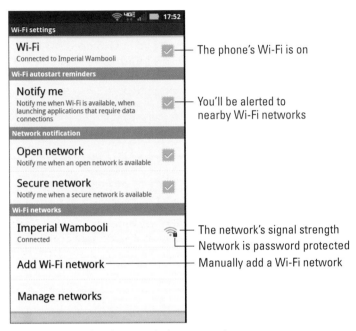

The phone's Wi-Fi is on

You'll be alerted to nearby Wi-Fi networks

The network's signal strength
Network is password protected
Manually add a Wi-Fi network

Figure 13-1: Hunting down a wireless network.

4. Choose a wireless network from the list.

In Figure 13-1, I'm using the Imperial Wambooli network, which is my office network.

5. If prompted, type the network password.

Putting a green check mark in the box by Show Password makes it easier to type a long, complex network password.

If the Wi-Fi network supports the WPS setup, you can connect by using the network PIN, pressing the connection button on the wireless router, or using whatever other WPS method is used by the router.

6. Touch the Connect button.

You should be immediately connected to the network. If not, try the password again.

When the phone is connected, you see the Wi-Fi status icon (shown in the margin) atop the touchscreen. This icon means that the phone's Wi-Fi is on, connected, and communicating with a Wi-Fi network.

Some wireless networks don't broadcast their names, which adds security but also makes accessing them more difficult. In these cases, choose the Add Wi-Fi Network command (refer to Figure 13-1) to manually add the network. You need to input the network name, or *SSID,* and the type of security. You also need the password, if one is used. You can obtain this information from the dour young man with the jet black hair and interesting neck tattoo who sold you coffee or from whoever is in charge of the wireless network at your location.

✔ Not every wireless network has a password.

✔ Some public networks are open to anyone, but you have to use the Browser app to get on the web and find a login page that lets you access the network. Simply browse to any page on the Internet and the login page shows up.

✔ The phone automatically remembers any Wi-Fi network it's connected to as well as its network password. The network is automatically connected as soon as the Droid 4 is within range.

✔ To disconnect from a Wi-Fi network, simply turn off Wi-Fi on the phone. See the preceding section.

✔ A Wi-Fi network is faster than the 3G cellular data network, so it makes sense to connect by Wi-Fi if the only other network available is 3G.

 ✔ Unlike a cellular data network, a Wi-Fi network's broadcast signal has a limited range. My advice is to use Wi-Fi when you plan to remain in one location for a while. If you wander too far away, your phone will lose the signal and be disconnected.

Knowing where you are with GPS

The Droid 4 communicates wirelessly with Global Positioning System (GPS) satellites in orbit around the Earth. The phone uses that information to help pinpoint your location, which comes in handy for the Maps app, the Navigation app, as well as other apps that need to know where you are.

You were prompted to turn on GPS services, also known as location services, when you first set up the Droid 4. To confirm that those services are on and active, follow these steps:

1. **At the Home screen, press the Menu soft button.**

2. **Choose the Settings command.**

3. **Choose Location & Security.**

   Five settings on the Location & Security Settings screen work with or augment the GPS wireless radio inside the Droid 4:

   - **E911 Only:** This service is used by emergency responders to locate your position. It cannot be disabled.

   - **Google Location Services:** This service uses certain Google tricks, such as the location of nearby Wi-Fi networks, to help augment and hone in on your location.

   - **Standalone GPS Services:** This service uses the GPS satellites, but it's not as strong or accurate as a handheld GPS gizmo. Therefore, it needs to be augmented by the Google Location and VZW Location services.

   - **VZW Location Services:** This is the Verizon service (VZW stands for Verizon Wireless) that helps find your location based on triangulation with the phone company's cell towers.

   - **Share Picture Location:** This option stores the location information, or geo-tag, in digital pictures taken on the phone.

4. **Set the GPS and location options by touching the square next to an item to turn it off or on.**

   An item is on when a green check mark is in the square.

I recommend keeping active all three primary location settings: Google Location Services, Standalone GPS Services, and VZW Location Services. The Share Picture Location item is nice but not necessary to finding out where you are.

A Connection to Share

That digital cellular signal sure is something. You and your Droid 4 can get on the Internet and do all those wonderful Internetty things anywhere the phone gets its digital cellular signal. Often times, those locations are places where Wi-Fi isn't available, so other devices — game machines, laptops, and desktop computers — just sit there and seethe with jealousy.

No electronic gizmo has a reason to harbor jealousy because your Droid 4 can readily and happily share its digital cellular Internet connection. The Droid 4 can share in two ways. The first method is to create a mobile hotspot, which allows any Wi-Fi–enabled device to access the Internet through your phone. The second method involves a direct connection between your phone and another device, which is a concept called *tethering*.

Creating a mobile hotspot

The mobile hotspot feature allows your Droid 4 to share its cellular data connection by creating its own Wi-Fi network. Other Wi-Fi devices — computers, laptops, other mobile devices — can then access that Wi-Fi network, enjoying a free ride on the Internet courtesy of your Droid 4.

Well, it may not be free. More on that later.

To set up a mobile hotspot with your phone, heed these steps:

1. **Turn off the Wi-Fi radio.**

   There's no point in creating a Wi-Fi hotspot where one is already available.

2. **Plug the phone into a power source.**

   The mobile hotspot feature draws a lot of power.

3. **From the Apps menu, open the Mobile Hotspot app.**

   Upon opening the app, you may see text describing the process. If so, dismiss the text.

4. **Place a green check mark next to the Mobile Hotspot item by touching its box.**

5. **Touch the OK button to dismiss the warning.**

6. **If you're prompted, accept the terms and conditions to subscribe to the service that gives your phone mobile hotspot capabilities.**

   On my phone, the fee is about $30 a month. That fee is in addition to my regular data plan.

7. **Name your mobile hotspot and change the password, if you so desire.**

   If you haven't set up a mobile hotspot yet, you need to supply some information, such as the name of your hotspot and the password. You can change the provided name and password or just keep them.

> Make a note of the password. You'll need it to log in to the mobile hotspot.

8. **Touch the OK button or the Save button to save your settings and start the hotspot.**

   You're done.

When the mobile hotspot is active, you see the Hotspot Active notification icon, similar to what's shown in the margin. You can then access the hotspot by using any computer or mobile device that has Wi-Fi capabilities.

To turn off the mobile hotspot, open the Mobile Hotspot app and remove the green check mark.

- The range for the mobile hotspot is about 30 feet. Things such as walls and antimatter can interfere with the signal, rendering it much shorter.

- Data usage fees apply when you use the mobile hotspot, and they're on top of the fee your cellular provider may charge for the basic service. Those fees can add up quickly.

- Don't forget to turn off the mobile hotspot when you're done using it.

Tethering the Internet connection

A more intimate and direct way to share the Droid 4's digital cellular connection is to connect the phone directly to a computer and activate the tethering feature.

Yes: I am fully aware that tethering goes against the wireless theme of this chapter. Still, it remains a solid way to provide Internet access to another gizmo, such as a laptop or desktop computer. Follow these steps to set up Internet tethering:

1. **Disable Wi-Fi.**

   You cannot tether the Wi-Fi connection, and the phone won't let you complete these steps with Wi-Fi on, so disable it. Directions are found in the "Activating Wi-Fi" section, earlier in the chapter.

2. **Connect the Droid 4 to another mobile device by using the USB cable.**

3. **On the phone, at the Home screen, press the Menu soft button.**

4. **Choose Settings, and then choose Wireless & Networks.**

5. **Choose Tethering & Mobile Hotspot.**

6. **Place a green check mark by the item USB Tethering.**

   Internet tethering is activated.

The other device should instantly recognize the phone as a "modem" with Internet access. Further configuration may be required, which depends on the device using the tethered connection. For example, the PC may prompt you to locate and install software for your phone. Do so: Accept the installation of new software when prompted by Windows.

Sharing the digital network connection incurs data usage charges against your cellular data plan. Be mindful of your data usage when you're sharing a connection.

The Bluetooth Way

Yet another type of computer network you can confuse yourself with is Bluetooth. It has nothing to do with the color blue or dental hygiene.

Bluetooth is a wireless protocol for communication between two or more Bluetooth-equipped devices. Your Droid 4 just happens to be Bluetooth-equipped, so it too can chat it up with Bluetooth devices, such as those earphone speakers that make you look like you have a stapler stuck to your ear.

Activating Bluetooth

You must turn on the phone's Bluetooth networking before you can use one of those Borg-earpiece implants and join the ranks of walking nerds. Here's how to turn on Bluetooth:

1. **At the Home screen, press the Menu soft button.**

2. **Choose Settings and then choose Wireless & Networks.**

3. **Choose Bluetooth.**

   Or, if a little green check mark already appears by the Bluetooth option, Bluetooth is already on.

To turn off Bluetooth, repeat the steps in this section; when you choose Bluetooth in Step 3, you'll be turning it off.

- ✔ When Bluetooth is on, the Bluetooth status icon appears, as shown in the margin.

- ✔ You can use the Toggle: Bluetooth widget to quickly turn on and off the Bluetooth radio. Refer to Chapter 15 for information on adding widgets to the Home screen.

- ✔ Activating Bluetooth can quickly drain the phone's battery. I recommend using Bluetooth only when necessary and turning it off when you're done.

Using a Bluetooth headset

Bluetooth can be used to pair the phone with a variety of gizmos, including your computer (if it's Bluetooth-equipped) and even Bluetooth printers, as described later in this chapter. Even so, the most common Bluetooth gizmo to use with a cell phone is a wireless headset.

To make the Bluetooth connection between your phone and a set of those I'm-so-cool earphones, follow these steps:

1. **Ensure that Bluetooth is on.**

2. **Turn on the Bluetooth headset.**

3. **At the Home screen, press the Menu soft button and choose Settings.**

4. **Choose Wireless & Networks and then choose Bluetooth Settings.**

   The Bluetooth Settings screen appears.

5. **Choose Scan for Devices.**

6. **If necessary, press the main button on the Bluetooth gizmo.**

   The main button is the one you use to answer the phone. You may have to press and hold down the button. Eventually, a picture of the device or its code number appears on the screen.

7. **Choose the device.**

8. **If necessary input the device's passcode.**

   The passcode is usually a four-digit number, and quite often it's simply 1234 or 0000.

When the device is connected, you can stick it in your ear and press its main Answer button when the phone rings.

After you've answered the call (by pressing the main Answer button on the earphone), you can chat away.

If you tire of using the Bluetooth headset, you can touch the Bluetooth button on the touchscreen to use the phone's own speaker and microphone. (Refer to Chapter 4 for the location of the Bluetooth button.)

✓ You can turn on and off the Bluetooth earphone after it's been paired. As long as the Droid 4's Bluetooth radio is on, the phone instantly recognizes the earphone when you turn it on.

✓ To unpair a device, locate it on the Bluetooth Settings screen. Then long-press the device and choose either the Disconnect or the Disconnect & Unpair command.

✓ Don't forget to turn off the earpiece when you're done with it. The earpiece has a battery, and it continues to drain when you forget to turn off the earpiece.

Fun with Wireless Printing

Here's something that might make you laugh: printing from a cell phone. But don't laugh, because printing on your Droid 4 is entirely possible. And don't cry either, because the various methods described in this section make the process a lot easier than you can imagine.

Printing to a Bluetooth printer

Of the various ways you can print something with your Droid 4, the most insane method is to print to a Bluetooth printer. I call it "insane" because it involves quite a few steps, not to mention that Bluetooth printers are kind of rare. Still, if you have a Bluetooth printer and are willing to risk your sanity and follow my suggestions, you'll be successful.

Before you can print, ensure that your Droid 4 is paired with a Bluetooth printer. Refer to the section "Using a Bluetooth headset," earlier in this chapter. Pairing a printer works exactly like pairing a headset: You need to make the printer discoverable and possibly type the printer's passcode on your phone to complete the connection.

You may also need to make the Droid 4 discoverable to get it connected to the printer. On the Bluetooth Settings screen, choose the Discoverable item. Then direct the printer to search for Bluetooth devices. Choose the Droid 4 on the printer's control panel to pair it with the phone.

When the printer and the Bluetooth printer are properly paired, you see the printer listed under Bluetooth Devices on the Bluetooth Settings screen, as shown in Figure 13-2. Even if it says Paired but Not Connected as it does in the figure, you're ready to go.

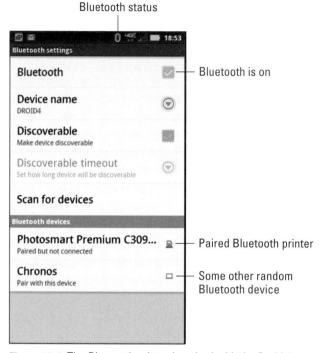

Figure 13-2: The Bluetooth printer is paired with the Droid 4.

Assuming that the Bluetooth printer is on and ready to print, obey these steps to print something on your Droid 4 phone by using the Share command:

1. **View the document, web page, or image you want to print.**

2. **Choose the Share command.**

    If a Share button isn't visible in the app, press the Menu soft button to look for the Share command.

3. **Choose Bluetooth from either the Share menu or the Share Via menu.**

   When no Bluetooth option is available, printing the item using Bluetooth isn't a possibility.

4. **Choose your Bluetooth printer from the list of items on the Bluetooth Device Picker screen.**

5. **If a prompt appears on the printer, confirm that the phone is printing a document.**

   The document is uploaded (sent from the phone to the printer), and then it prints. You can view the upload status by pulling down the phone's notifications.

 ↙ Bluetooth printers sport the Bluetooth logo somewhere.

 ↙ When printing images from the My Gallery app, I recommend loading up the printer with photo paper for the best results. You can obtain photo paper at any computer or office supply store.

Printing with MOTOPRINT

The Droid 4 comes with the wireless network printing app MOTOPRINT. You can use this app to print from your phone to any wireless printer on a Wi-Fi network. Follow these steps:

1. **Ensure that your Droid 4 is connected to a Wi-Fi network.**

   The network should have a network printer available for sharing, either a standalone network printer or a printer on a network computer that's been made available for sharing.

2. **Start the MOTOPRINT app.**

   The first time you start MOTOPRINT, you see some information displayed. Feel free to touch the Continue button.

3. **Choose something to print from the MOTOPRINT menu.**

   For example, to print a saved Gmail message, choose the Saved Emails option.

4. **Browse for the item to print.**

   When no items to print are available, you're rudely informed. Try another category or use another printing method.

5. **If prompted by the Complete Action Using menu, choose the command Print with MOTOPRINT.**

6. **Choose your printer from the Favorites list or touch the Add Printers button to locate a wireless printer.**

   Steps 7–10 assume that the Favorites list is empty. Skip to Step 11 if you find your printer on the Favorites list.

7. **Choose the At Home or At Work option, depending on where you're printing.**

8. **Choose the Find Printers option.**

   Eventually, you'll see the Printers screen populated with available network printers.

9. **Choose a printer from the list.**

   The Droid 4 confirms that the printer is available for printing. If so, a green check mark appears by the printer's name.

10. **Touch the Save button.**

    The printer is added to the Favorites list.

11. **Choose the printer to use from the list.**

12. **Choose optional printer settings on the Print screen.**

    You can set the number of copies and choose the paper size and other options, just as you would when printing from Windows, for example.

13. **Touch the Print button.**

    The item is queued up and printed.

The MOTOPRINT command is available from other apps, such as Gmail and the Gallery. If the command doesn't appear on the screen, press the Menu soft button and look for either the Print or MOTOPRINT command.

- ✔ Printing options are available also on the various Share menus on the Droid 4, though the option may not exist for all document types or in all apps.

- ✔ Printing with MOTOPRINT is faster than Bluetooth printing.

- ✔ The option to choose whether the Wi-Fi printer is at home or work (Step 7) probably has more to do with network security than the phone really caring where you are.

Sharing with the Print to Retail option

Unlike other options in this section, Print to Retail doesn't send a document or an image to a printer near you. Well, *near you* as in the same room or building. No, what the Print to Retail option does is send the document or image to a local photo developer, such as Costco.

After you choose the Print to Retail option from the Share command menu, the Droid 4 uses its GPS capabilities to locate nearby retail photo developers. You can choose one of them and then fill in the blanks to begin the printing process. Your pictures are eventually sent electronically to the developer and printed. They're available for payment and pickup later.

Everywhere but in the Air

The Droid 4's wireless features enhance the phone's capability to be free, unfettered, and utterly mobile. But most of those wireless capabilities are unwanted in one common situation: when you travel aboard an airplane.

As an airplane takes off, passengers are admonished to turn off their cell phones. Do so. Further, if you use the phone in the air, you're told to disable its wireless radios: Those wireless radios control the phone's capabilities to make calls, access the digital cellular network, GPS, Bluetooth, and other wireless wonders. To disable all those things in one action, and make your phone safe for air travel, you place the Droid 4 into what's commonly called *airplane mode*.

 The fastest way to switch the phone to airplane mode is to press and hold the Power Lock button. From the Phone Options menu, choose Airplane Mode.

You can manually enter airplane mode by following these tedious steps:

1. **At the Home screen, press the Menu soft button.**
2. **Choose Settings.**
3. **Choose Wireless & Networks.**
4. **Touch the gray box by Airplane Mode to place a green check mark there.**

    The phone is in airplane mode.

When the Droid 4 is airplane mode, an Airplane Mode status icon (shown in the margin) appears at the top of the touchscreen.

To disable airplane mode — after the plane has landed and the flight crew has informed you that it's safe to do so — repeat the steps in this section but in Step 4 remove the green check mark.

- ✔ Even with your Droid 4 in airplane mode, it's possible to turn on the phone's Wi-Fi capabilities. Although you can't access any ground-based networks, many airlines do offer in-flight Wi-Fi service. A flat rate applies, but the expense is worthwhile if you need to keep in touch in the air.

- ✔ I just leave my phone off the entire time I fly or place it in sleep mode. See Chapter 1 for information on sleep mode.

Chapter 14

Share and Synchronize

You can get information into your Droid 4 in many ways. You can type on the keyboard. You can download information from the Internet. People can send you things. What's left? The job of sharing and synchronizing information between your phone and a computer. That job is handled by the USB connection, which can get information not only into your phone but also out. This important topic is covered in this chapter.

The USB Connection

The most direct way to mate your Droid 4 with a computer is to use a USB cable. Coincidentally, a USB cable comes with the phone. It's a match made in heaven but, like many matches, it often works less than smoothly. Rather than hire a counselor to get the phone and computer on speaking terms, I offer you some good USB connection advice in this section.

Connecting the phone to a computer

You can try rubber bands, Velcro, or even chewing gum to connect your Droid 4 to your computer, but the proper way is to use the

USB cable. The cable's A end plugs into the computer. The other end, known as the *micro-USB connector,* plugs into the phone's USB hole.

Computer nerds call the USB hole a *port.*

The cable plugs in only one way, so you can't connect the computer and phone improperly, backwards, or upside down. That's good.

When your phone is connected via a USB cable to a computer, the USB Connection notification icon appears, similar to what's shown in the margin. Refer to the next section to see what you can do with this notification to configure the USB connection.

✔ If possible, plug the USB cable into the computer itself, not into a USB hub. The phone-computer connection works best with a powered USB port.

✔ A flurry of activity takes place when you first connect your Droid 4 phone to a Windows PC. Notifications pop up about new software that's installed, or you may see the AutoPlay dialog box, prompting you to install software. Do so.

Configuring the USB connection

Upon successful connection of your Droid 4 to a computer, you have the option of configuring the USB connection. A menu appears, either automatically or when you choose the USB notification, as shown in Figure 14-1.

Figure 14-1: A USB Connection menu.

Here's a description of the options:

- ✔ **PC Mode:** Don't choose this option.

- ✔ **Windows Media Sync:** This option is used on a Windows PC to treat the phone as a media device, similar to a camera or a MP3 music player. This option is ideal for synchronizing files.

- ✔ **USB Mass Storage:** When this option is chosen, the computer treats the Droid 4 like a removable storage device, such as a USB thumb drive or a media card.

- ✔ **Charge Only:** Use this option when you want to only charge the phone and not have it communicate with the computer. Because there is no data connection, the Charge Only option may be titled None on some phones.

Make your choice, and then touch the OK button to make the connection. Or when you choose Charge Only, the phone doesn't talk with the computer but uses the USB connection to charge its battery.

- ✔ On a Windows 7 computer, when you connect the Droid 4 using the Windows Media Sync setting, you'll see a device window. That window pops up automatically, and it makes synchronizing information a snap. Refer to Chapter 11 to see what the device window looks like.

- ✔ If you have a Macintosh, use the Charge Only and USB Mass Storage settings. Other options may not be compatible with the Mac.

- ✔ The PC Mode option works on some Windows PCs to identify the Droid 4 using the Media Transfer Protocol (MTP). I've never gotten it to work. The Windows Media Sync and USB Mass Storage options should serve all your needs.

- ✔ After choosing the Media Sync or Mass Storage option, you see one or two AutoPlay dialog boxes on your Windows PC. You can choose how to deal with the phone by using this dialog box to choose an item such as Open Folder to View Files or Windows Media Player. Or just close the dialog box.

- ✔ The reason you may see two AutoPlay dialog boxes is that most Android phones feature two storage locations: internal storage and the microSD card. One AutoPlay dialog box appears for each storage location.

- ✔ No matter which USB connection option you've chosen, the phone's battery charges when it's connected to a computer's USB port — as long as the computer is turned on, of course.

> ✔ You may not be able to access the phone's storage while it's mounted onto a computer storage system. Items such as your music and photos are unavailable until you disconnect the phone from the computer or choose the Charge Only (None) setting for the USB connection.

Disconnecting the phone from the computer

When you're using any USB connection option other than Charge Only, you must properly disconnect the phone from the computer. Never just yank out the USB cable. Never! Never! Never! Doing so can damage the phone's storage, which is a Bad Thing. Instead, follow these steps to do things properly:

1. **Close whichever programs or windows are accessing the Droid 4 from your computer.**

2. **Properly unmount the phone from the computer's storage system.**

   On a PC, locate the phone's icon in the Computer or My Computer window. Right-click the icon and choose either the Eject or Safely Remove command.

   On a Macintosh, drag the phone's storage icon(s) to the trash.

3. **On your Droid 4, pull down the notifications.**

4. **Choose USB Connection.**

5. **Choose the Charge Only setting.**

6. **Touch the OK button to confirm.**

   The phone's storage is unmounted and can no longer be accessed from your computer.

7. **If you like, unplug the USB cable.**

When you choose to keep the phone connected to the computer, the phone continues to charge. (Only when the computer is off does the phone not charge.) Otherwise, the computer and phone have ended their little *tête-à-tête* and you and your Droid 4 are once again free again to wander the earth.

Synchronize Your Stuff

The synchronizing procedure involves hooking your Droid 4 to a computer and then swapping information back and forth. This process can be done automatically by using special software or manually by using your brain and some sweat.

Synchronizing with doubleTwist

The Droid 4 doesn't come with any specific synchronization software. Well, maybe the Backup Assistant, but I've never used that program and it scares me to death. So I recommend using the world's most popular Android phone synchronization program, a nifty utility called doubleTwist.

The doubleTwist program is free. It's for your computer, not your phone. You can download a copy from the doubleTwist website at `www.doubletwist.com`.

You use doubleTwist to synchronize pictures, music, videos, and web page subscriptions between your computer and its media libraries and any portable device, such as your phone. Additionally, doubleTwist gives you the ability to search the Google Play Store and obtain new apps for your phone.

To use doubleTwist, connect your phone to your computer with a USB cable, as described earlier in this chapter. Choose either that Mass Storage or Media Sync option; the phone's internal storage and microSD card are added to your computer's storage system as a USB mass storage device.

Start up the doubleTwist program if it doesn't start by itself. The simple doubleTwist interface is shown in Figure 14-2.

The way I use doubleTwist is to drag and drop media either from my computer to the phone or the other way around. Use the program's interface to browse for media, as shown in Figure 14-2.

✔ You do not need to upgrade to doubleTwist Airsync if you don't want to. It's not a necessary requirement for using the doubleTwist program.

✔ If you choose a Media Sync option, only the phone's microSD card is available in doubleTwist, as shown in Figure 14-2. When you choose the Mass Storage connection option, both the internal and microSD storage areas are available.

✓ You cannot copy media purchased at the iTunes store from the Mac to your Droid 4. Apparently, you need to upgrade to iTunes Plus before the operation is allowed.

✓ doubleTwist doesn't synchronize contact information. Contact information is automatically synchronized between your phone's address book and Google. For synchronizing vCards, see the next section.

✓ Information on synchronizing music between your computer and phone is covered in Chapter 11.

Items stored on your computer   Choose what to sync

Drag items to the phone

Items stored on the phone

Figure 14-2: The doubleTwist synchronization utility.

Doing a manual sync

When you can't get software on your computer to synchronize automatically, you have to resort to doing the old manual connection. Yes, it can be complex. And bothersome. And tedious. But a manual sync is often the only way to get some information out of the phone and on to a computer, or vice versa.

Follow these steps to copy files between your computer and your Droid 4:

1. **Connect the phone to the computer by using the USB cable.**

2. **Choose the USB Mass Storage option for the USB connection.**

   Specific directions are offered earlier in this chapter.

3a. **On a PC, in the AutoPlay dialog box, choose the option Open Folder to View Files.**

   The option might instead read Open Device to View Files.

   If your Droid 4 has a microSD card installed, you will see two AutoPlay dialog boxes: MOT is the phone's internal storage; NO NAME is the microSD card (removable) storage.

   After choosing to open the folder (or device), you see a folder window appear, which looks like any common folder in Windows. The difference is that the files and folders in this window are on the phone, not on your computer.

3b. **On a Macintosh, open the removable drive icon(s) to access the phone's storage.**

   The Mac uses generic, removable drive icons to represent the phone's storage. If two icons appear, one represents the phone's internal storage, and the second is for the phone's microSD card or removable storage.

4. **Open a folder window on your computer.**

   You should open either the folder from which you're copying files to the phone or the folder that will receive files from the phone— for example, the `Documents` or `My Documents` folder.

   If you're copying files from the phone to your computer, use the `Pictures` folder for pictures and videos and the `Documents` folder for everything else.

5. **Drag the file icons from one folder window to the other to copy them between the phone and computer.**

   Use Figure 14-3 as your guide.

6. **When you're done, properly unmount the phone's storage from your computer's storage system and disconnect the USB cable.**

   You must eject the phone's storage icon(s) from the Macintosh computer before you can turn off USB storage on the phone.

Drag files to here to copy to root

Droid 4 internal storage is drive H on this PC

Droid 4 microSD storage is drive I on this PC

Files on your computer

Files on the Droid 4

Specific folders on the phone

Figure 14-3: Copying files to the phone.

Any files you've copied to the phone are now stored either on the phone's internal storage or on the microSD card. What you do with those files next depends on the reasons you copied the files: to view pictures, use the Gallery; to import vCards, use the Contacts app; to listen to music, use the Music Player; and so on.

✔ It doesn't matter to which storage location you copy files — internal storage or microSD card (removable storage). I recommend using the microSD card because the phone seems to prioritize its internal storage and can fill up quickly.

✔ Quite a few files can be found in the *root folder,* the main folder on the phone's microSD card, which you see when the phone is mounted onto your computer's storage system and you open its folder.

✔ A good understanding of basic file operations is necessary to get the most benefit from transferring files between your computer and the phone. These basic operations include copying, moving, renaming, and deleting. Being familiar with the concept of folders also helps. A doctorate in entanglement theory is optional.

Finding files on your phone

Like other devices that use storage, your Droid 4 has a penchant for organization. Unlike your typical teenage male, the phone doesn't just leave files laying all over the floor. The Droid 4 has special places where it stores certain files. If you want to manually synchronize files, or just go file spelunking on your phone, knowing where things are stored helps.

Here are some common locations for popular files on your phone:

- ✔ /download: This folder contains files you've downloaded using the Browser app or files that may have been transferred into the phone from the Internet or by an e-mail attachment.

- ✔ /dcim/Camera: Pictures and videos are stored in this folder.

- ✔ /Music : The Play Music app organizes your phone's music into this folder. Subfolders are organized by artist.

These folders can exist in internal storage or the microSD card. So when you can't find the file or folder you're looking for on one media, look in the other.

- ✔ To peruse a list of files you've downloaded on your Droid 4, open the Downloads app. It lists the contents of the download folder, but in an entirely human-readable format.

- ✔ If you truly adore computer file management, you can use the My Files app to explore the Droid 4's storage system. The app works similarly to file management programs on computers, so if you understand such a thing you'll feel right at home.

The HDMI Connection

Nestled on the Droid 4's left flank is a hole labeled HDMI. That hole is the phone's HDMI connector, which lets you pump out the touchscreen's display to a full-size (or larger) HDMI computer monitor or television set. That way, you can watch a video, view a slideshow, or play Cut the Rope on a full-size screen instead of the Droid 4's diminutive, pocket-sized display.

HDMI stands for High Definition Multimedia Interface.

Here are the specific steps for doing the HDMI thing with your Droid 4:

1. **Attach the HDMI cable to the HDMI monitor or TV set.**

   If the TV is an HDMI TV, make a note of the port number so that you can switch to that input channel for viewing the phone.

2. **Plug the HDMI cable into the Droid 4's HDMI jack.**

   Yes, the jack looks a lot like micro-USB connector, which is right next door. Getting the two connectors confused happens often.

3. **Choose which option you want for HDMI viewing using the Select Dock Type menu.**

   Here are your choices:

   - **My Gallery:** Opens the My Gallery app. You can start a slideshow by choosing My Library, opening an album, and then pressing the Menu soft button and choosing the Slideshow command.

   - **Music:** Starts the My Music app, which is the Android Music player, not the Google Play Music app. Choose My Library, and then find an album, or an artist and enjoy watching the My Music app on the big screen. (The sound should play from the HDMI monitor or TV's speakers, if it has built-in speakers.)

   - **Mirror On Display:** Duplicates the Droid 4 screen output on the HDMI TV or monitor. Choose this option when you want to watch a rented movie full-size.

4. **On the HDMI monitor, choose whichever command switches input to the Droid 4.**

   You may have to use the remote control to switch the input.

5. **Disconnect the HDMI cable when you're done.**

   You don't have to give any commands or touch a button; just unplug the cable.

 If you change your mind about your choice in Step 3, pull down the notifications and choose the item Connected to HDMI Cable. Then choose another option from the menu.

Chapter 15

Customize

Customizing a cell phone isn't like customizing a car. You're not going to give your Droid 4 a paint job. You're not going to add a spoiler. There's nowhere you can attach a chrome-plated exhaust. So what's left? Changing the way the phone looks and behaves. The process isn't as difficult as it sounds.

Although many people prefer the uninspired consistency of the phone as it's preconfigured, you may be one of the few who desire more. By customizing your phone, you make it your own. This chapter shows you a few things you can do to make the Droid 4 look and work the way you want it to.

Home Screen Improvement

The key to changing the Droid 4 Home screen is the *long-press.* Press and hold your finger on a blank part of the Home screen (not on an icon). You see the Add to Home menu appear, as shown in Figure 15-1. From the menu, you can begin your Home screen customization adventure, as discussed in this section.

When the Add to Home menu doesn't show up, that Home screen panel is already full of icons or widgets. Swipe the screen to another Home screen panel and try again.

Figure 15-1: The Add to Home menu.

Hanging new wallpaper

You can hang two types of *wallpapers,* or backgrounds, on the Home screen: traditional and live. *Live wallpapers* are animated. A not-so-live wallpaper can be any image, such as a picture taken with the Droid 4's camera.

To set the Home screen wallpaper, obey these steps:

1. **Long-press the Home screen.**

   The Add to Home Screen menu appears (refer to Figure 15-1).

2. **Choose the Wallpapers command.**

3. **Choose the wallpaper you want from the list.**

   Your choices are

   - **Live Wallpapers:** Animated or interactive wallpapers

   - **My Gallery:** Still images stored in the My Gallery app

   - **Wallpapers:** Wallpapers from a range of stunning images preinstalled by the phone's manufacturer

   For the My Gallery option, you see a preview of the wallpaper where you can select and crop part of the image.

   For certain live wallpapers, the Settings button may appear. The settings let you customize certain aspects of the interactive wallpaper.

4. **Touch the Save, Set Wallpaper, or Apply button to confirm your selection.**

   The new wallpaper takes over the Home screen.

Live wallpaper is interactive, usually featuring some form of animation. Otherwise, the wallpaper image scrolls slightly as you swipe
from one Home screen panel to another.

> ✔ If you need to change the wallpaper and all the Home screen
> panels are full of icons, press the Menu soft button and
> choose the Wallpaper command.
>
> ✔ To restore the Droid 4's original wallpaper, choose Wallpapers
> in Step 3, and then touch the Reset to Default button.
>
> ✔ The Zedge app has some interesting wallpaper features. You
> can obtain the Zedge app at the Google Play Store, which is
> covered in Chapter 12.

Adding an app

Those apps that Verizon or Motorola stuck on the Droid 4's
Home screen need not be the only apps to dwell there. Indeed,
you can even evict those apps, as discussed in the later section,
"Rearranging and removing icons and widgets." To add your own
favorite or popular apps, just follow these steps:

1. **Visit the Home screen panel on which you want to stick
   the app icon shortcut.**

   The screen must have room for the icon shortcut.

2. **Touch the Apps icon to display the Apps menu.**

3. **Long-press the icon of the app you want to add to the
   Home screen.**

4. **Choose the command Add to Home.**

   A copy of the app's icon is placed on the Home screen.

The app hasn't moved: What you see is a copy or, officially, a *shortcut.* You can still find the app on the Apps menu, but now the app
is available — more conveniently — on the Home screen.

Sticking an app on the dock

The *dock* sits at the bottom of every Home screen panel and is
composed of three app icons — Phone, Text, Camera — plus the
Apps icon. I don't recommend changing the Phone icon, and you
can't replace Apps. To replace the Text or Camera apps on the
dock, follow these steps:

1. **Long-press the dock icon you want to replace.**

   Long-press for only a brief moment, and then release your finger.

2. **Choose the new app from the list.**

   The new app icon is stuck to the dock, replacing the app icon you long-pressed in Step 1.

It's not possible to remove a dock icon and replace it with nothing.

 You can also drag an icon from the Home screen to the dock, as covered in the later section, "Rearranging and removing icons and widgets."

Decorating with widgets

Just like app icons, the Home screen can be festooned with *widgets,* or tiny, interactive information windows. A widget often provides a gateway into another app, or displays information such as status updates, the currently playing song, or the weather. To add a widget to the Home screen, heed these steps:

1. **Switch to a Home screen panel that has room enough for the new widget.**

   Unlike app icons, some widgets can occupy more than a postage-stamp-size piece of real estate on the Home screen.

2. **Long-press the Home screen and choose the Widgets command.**

3. **From the list, choose the widget you want to add.**

   For example, choose a toggle widget to get quick access to several popular phone features, such as Wi-Fi or Bluetooth or other settings you often turn on or off.

The widget is plopped on the Home screen.

The variety of available widgets depends on the applications you've installed. Some applications come with widgets; some don't.

 ✔ The Toggle: Power Control widget contains on-off buttons for several popular phone features: Wi-Fi, Bluetooth, GPS, Google Sync, and Auto Brightness.

✔ More widgets are available at the Google Play Store (see Chapter 12).

✔ To remove, move, or rearrange a widget, see the next section.

Rearranging and removing icons and widgets

Stars may be fixed in the heavens, but the icons and widgets on your Droid 4 Home screen aren't fastened using anything stronger than digital bubble gum. My point is that it's relatively easy to drag icons and widgets around or remove them altogether.

The secret to moving an app shortcut or widget is to long-press its icon on the Home screen. The icon seems to lift and break free, as shown in Figure 15-2.

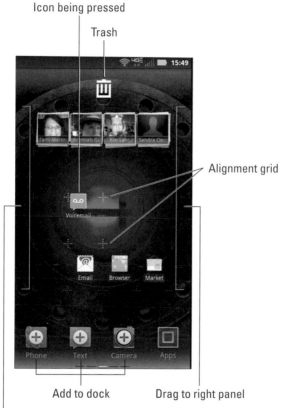

Icon being pressed

Trash

Alignment grid

Add to dock   Drag to right panel

Drag to left panel

Figure 15-2: Moving an icon.

You can drag a free icon to another position on the Home screen or to another Home screen panel, or you can drag it to the Trash icon that appears on the Home screen, which deletes the shortcut.

Widgets are moved or removed in the same manner as icons.

- Dragging a Home screen icon or widget to the Trash removes from the Home screen the icon or widget but doesn't uninstall it. The app can still be found on the Apps menu, and the widget can once again be added to the Home screen.

- When you hover an icon over the Trash icon, ready to delete the icon, its color changes to red.

- See Chapter 12 for information on uninstalling applications.

Add Some Security

The Droid 4's lock screen is a simple gizmo that anyone can pick; slide the unlock button to the right and you instantly gain access to the phone's information and features. For most folks, that simple lock is secure enough. For others, the lock is about as effective as fighting a forest fire with a squirt gun.

You can supplement the Droid 4's basic screen lock with one of three additional types of security locks: pattern, PIN, or password. The details are provided in this section.

The lock doesn't show up!

The lock screen shows up whenever you turn on the phone or wake it up from sleep mode. Whether the lock appears after awakening the phone depends on how long the phone has been sleeping. If you awaken the phone right away, for example, the lock may not even show up. The timing depends on the Security Lock Timer setting.

The Security Lock Timer setting specifies how long the phone waits after being put to sleep before the screen lock appears. Initially, the timer is set to 20 minutes. You can set it to a shorter interval, which is more secure. From the Home screen, press the Menu soft button and choose Settings. Choose Location & Security, and then choose Security Lock Timer. Choose a new time-out value from the list.

Finding the screen locks

All the Droid 4's screen locks can be found on the Choose Screen Lock screen. Heed these steps to visit that screen:

1. **At the Home screen, press the Menu soft button.**

2. **Choose Settings.**

3. **Choose Location & Security.**

4. **If no additional lock is set, choose Set Up Screen Lock; otherwise, choose Change Screen Lock.**

If the screen lock is already set, you have to work the lock to proceed: Trace the pattern or type the PIN or password to continue. You then get access to the Screen Unlock Security screen, which shows four items: None, Pattern, PIN, and Password. Using those items is covered in the next few sections.

✔ The lock you apply affects the way you turn on and wake up your phone. See Chapter 1 for details.

✔ The locks don't appear when you answer an incoming phone call. You are prompted to unlock the phone, however, if you want to use its features while you're on a call.

✔ See the sidebar "The lock doesn't show up" for information on setting the Security Lock timer, which affects when the screen locks appear after you put the phone to sleep.

Removing a lock

To disable the pattern, PIN, or password screen lock on your phone, choose the None option from the Screen Unlock Security screen. When None is chosen, the phone uses the simple slide lock, as described in Chapter 1.

Creating an unlock pattern

The unlock pattern is perhaps the most popular, and certainly the most unconventional, way to lock your Droid 4. You must trace the pattern on the touchscreen to unlock the phone.

To set the unlock pattern, follow these steps:

1. **Summon the Screen Unlock Security screen.**

   Refer to the earlier section "Finding the screen locks."

2. **Choose Pattern.**

   If you haven't yet set a pattern, you may see a tutorial describing the process; touch the Next button to skip merrily through the dreary directions.

3. **Trace an unlock pattern.**

   Use Figure 15-3 as your guide. You can trace over the dots in any order, but you can trace over a dot only once. The pattern must cover at least four dots.

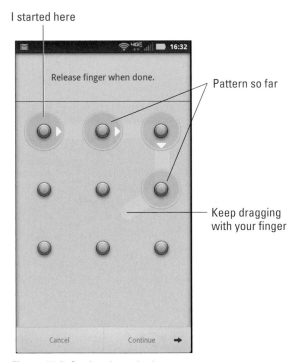

I started here

Release finger when done.

Pattern so far

Keep dragging with your finger

Figure 15-3: Setting the unlock pattern.

4. **Touch the Continue button.**

5. **Redraw the pattern again, just to confirm that you know it.**

6. **Touch the Confirm button and the pattern lock is set.**

Ensure that a check mark appears by the option Use Visible Pattern, found on the Location & Security Settings screen. That way, the grid of dots shows up when you need to unlock the phone. For even more security, you can disable this option, but you *must* remember how and where the pattern goes.

- ✔ To remove the pattern lock, set None as the lock type, as described in the preceding section.

- ✔ The pattern lock can start at any dot, not necessarily at the upper-left dot, shown in Figure 15-3.

- ✔ The unlock pattern can be as simple or as complex as you like. I'm a big fan of simple.

- ✔ Wash your hands! Smudge marks on the display can betray your pattern.

Setting a PIN

A *PIN lock* is a code containing 4 to 16 numbers, from 0 through 9. To set the PIN lock for your Droid 4, follow the directions in the earlier section "Finding the screen locks" to reach the Choose Screen Lock screen. Choose PIN from the list of locks.

Type your PIN twice to confirm to the doubting computer that you know it. The next time you need to unlock your phone, type the PIN on the keyboard and then touch the Enter key to proceed.

Figure 15-4 shows the PIN unlocking screen you'll see when you unlock your Droid 4. Before typing your PIN, you'll have to work the initial unlocking screen (slide the lock button to the right).

The onscreen keyboard (refer to Figure 15-4) doesn't appear if you've extended the Droid 4's sliding keyboard. In that case, use the sliding keyboard to type your PIN.

Applying a password

Perhaps the most secure way to lock the phone's screen is to apply a full-on password. Unlike a PIN (refer to the preceding section), a *password* contains a combination of numbers, symbols, and uppercase and lowercase letters.

Set the password by choosing Password from the Choose Screen Lock screen; refer to the earlier section "Finding the screen locks" for information on getting to that screen.

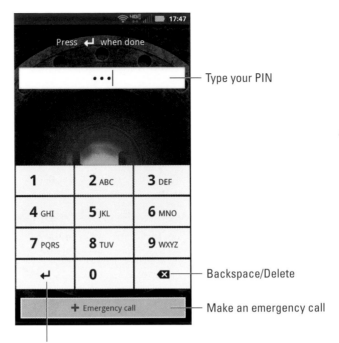

Touch the Enter key when done

Figure 15-4: Unlocking your Droid 4 with a PIN.

The password you create must be at least four characters. Longer passwords are more secure but easier to mistype.

To set things up, you type the password twice, which confirms to the phone that you know the password and will, you hope, remember it in the future.

The phone prompts you to type the password whenever you unlock the screen, as described in Chapter 1. You also type the password whenever you change or remove the screen lock, as discussed in the section "Finding the screen locks," earlier in this chapter.

Various Phone Adjustments

The number of items, settings, and options you can play with on the Droid 4 is nearly endless. Some adjustments fix annoying things; others might be interesting but unknown to you. I cover some of the more popular settings in this section.

Choosing a ringtone

To select a new ringtone for your Droid 4, or to simply confirm which ringtone you're using, follow these steps:

1. **At the Home screen, press the Menu soft button.**

2. **Choose Settings and then choose Sound.**

3. **Choose Phone Ringtone.**

   If you have a ringtone application, you may see a menu that asks you which source to use for the phone's ringtone. Choose Android System.

4. **Choose a ringtone from the list that's displayed.**

   Scroll through the list. Tap a ringtone to hear a preview.

5. **Touch OK to accept the new ringtone or touch Cancel to keep the phone's ringtone as is.**

You can also set the ringtone used for notifications. In Step 3, choose Notification Ringtone rather than Phone Ringtone.

✔ Text messaging ringtones are set from the Text Messaging app. See Chapter 11.

✔ You can set up ringtones specific to a contact. When viewing the contact's information, press the Menu soft button and choose Options, and then chose Ringtone. Select a ringtone from the list to assign that specific ringtone to the contact. See Chapter 5 for more information about contacts in your Droid 4.

✔ You can use any tune from your phone's music library as the phone's ringtone. To make this trick work, you have to play the tune using the My Music app. While playing a tune (or while it's paused), press the Menu soft button and choose More, then choose Use As Ringtone. That tune becomes the phone's main ringtone.

✔ Music you choose as a ringtone plays from the start of the song until you answer the phone.

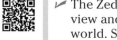

✔ The Zedge app has oodles of free ringtones available for preview and download, all shared by Android users around the world. See Chapter 12 for information about the Play Store and how to download and install apps such as Zedge on your phone.

Create your own ringtones

You can use as a ringtone for your phone any MP3 or WAV audio file, such as a personalized message, a sound you record on your computer, or an audio file you purloined from the Internet. As long as the sound is in the MP3 or WAV format, it can work as a ringtone on your Droid 4.

The secret to creating your own ringtone is to transfer the audio file from your computer to the phone. The topic of synchronizing files is covered in Chapter 14. After the audio file is in the phone's music library, you can choose the file as a ringtone in the same way you can assign any music on the phone as a ringtone, as described in the preceding section.

Stopping the noise

The Droid 4 sports a slew of tricks designed to control the noise it makes. These techniques can come in quite handy, especially when a cell phone's digital noise can be outright annoying.

Turning on vibration mode

You can make the phone vibrate for all incoming calls, which works in addition to any ringtone you've set (and still works when you've silenced the phone). To activate vibration all-the-time mode, follow these steps:

1. **At the Home screen, press the Menu soft button.**
2. **Choose Settings and then Sound.**
3. **Choose Vibrate.**
4. **Choose Always.**

When the Always option is chosen, the phone vibrates even when it's silenced. Speaking of which. . . .:

Setting silent mode

Silent mode disables all sounds from the phone, except for music and YouTube and other types of media, as well as alarms that have been set by the Alarm (or Clock) and Calendar apps.

To enter silent mode, follow Steps 1 and 2 in the preceding set of steps and then place a check mark by the item Silent Mode.

Adjusting the ringer volume

For the most precise way to preset the noise your Droid 4 makes, choose Sound and then choose Volume. Use the sliders to specify how loud the phone rings for incoming calls (ringtones), media, and alarms. If you place a check mark by the Notifications item, the Ringtone setting also applies to notifications. Touch OK when you're done.

Performing automatic phone tricks

You might find handy two helpful phone settings on the Droid 4: Auto Answer on Headset and Auto Retry. Both options are found on the Call Settings screen. At the Home screen, press the Menu soft button, choose Settings, and then choose the Call Settings item.

By placing a check mark by Auto Retry, you direct the phone to automatically redial a number when the call doesn't go through. Obviously, this feature is ideal for radio show call-in contests.

The Auto Answer on Headset option directs the Droid 4 to automatically answer the phone when a headset is attached. The option has three settings that specify how long to wait before the call is answered (2, 5, and 10 seconds). The fourth setting, Off, disables the feature.

Setting the double-tap Home soft button function

As master of your Droid 4, you can determine what happens when you press the Home soft button twice, a process known as the *double-tap Home launch* function. Out of the box, the Droid 4 (as least, my Droid 4) does nothing when you press the Home soft button twice quickly. You can change this behavior so that pressing the Home button twice does a variety of interesting or useful things.

To modify the double-tap Home launch function, heed these steps:

1. **At the Home screen, press the Menu soft button.**

2. **Choose Settings and then choose Applications.**

3. **Choose Double Tap Home Launch.**

4. **Choose a new function or app from the menu.**

   For example, you can choose Dialer to summon the Phone app whenever you press the Home button twice. Choose None to disable the double-tap Home launch feature.

 A handy option to choose for double-tap Home launch is Camera. I find this setting extremely useful, even more so than the Camera app's shortcut on the Home screen dock.

Using accessibility settings

If you find that the Droid 4 doesn't meet your physical needs, consider taking advantage of some of the phone's accessibility features. Follow these steps:

1. **While at the Home screen, press the Menu soft button.**

2. **Choose Settings and then choose Accessibility.**

3. **Place a check mark by the Accessibility option.**

   Two options become available when accessibility is on:

   • **Voice Readouts:** Touching items on the screen directs the phone to read that text.

   • **Zoom Mode:** A magnification window appears on the touchscreen, allowing you to better see teensy information.

4. **Touch the OK button after reading the scary warning.**

   The Accessibility feature is active.

To disable any accessibility settings, repeat these steps and remove check marks in Step 3. Or just deselect the Accessibility setting to disable them all. Touch OK to confirm.

Changing various settings

This section describes a smattering of settings you can adjust on the Droid 4 — all settings made from, logically, the Settings screen. To get there from the Home screen, press the Menu soft button and choose the Settings command.

You can view the Settings screen also by choosing the Settings app from the App menu.

✓ **Screen brightness:** Choose Display and then choose Brightness. The Automatic Brightness setting uses the phone's magical light sensor to determine the brightness at your location. If you disable this setting, you can move the slider on the screen to specify how bright the display appears.

✓ **Screen timeout:** Choose Display and then choose Screen Timeout. Select a time-out value from the list. This duration specifies when the phone locks and the touchscreen goes dark.

✓ **Call Connect:** Choose Sound and place a check mark by the option Call Connect. When a new call comes in, you hear a sound, alerting you to the new call. This option is especially helpful when you use the Droid 4 to listen to music.

✓ **Network Lost Tone:** Choose Sound and then place a check mark by the option Network Lost Tone. The Droid 4 plays a tone when a phone call is dropped because of a poor network connection.

✓ **Keep the phone awake when plugged in:** Choose Applications and then choose Development. Place a check mark by the option Stay Awake.

Chapter 16

Ten Tips, Tricks, and Shortcuts

I'd like to think that this book is packed with good advice and healthy tips on using your Droid 4. Yet, of all the good advice in this book, I believe that several items — ten to be exact — stand out. They are my ten favorite tips, tricks, and shortcuts, presented in this chapter.

Quick Launch

The sliding keyboard has 36 keys to which you can assign app shortcuts. That's 1 shortcut for every letter key, A through Z, plus 10 for the numbers 1 through 9 and 0. The keyboard shortcuts make up the Quick Launch function. Setting them up works like this:

1. **At the Home screen, press the Menu soft button.**

2. **Choose Settings, and then choose Applications.**

3. **Choose Quick Launch.**

   You see various entries titled Assign Application, followed by the 36 keys from the keyboard, A through Z, and then 0 through 9. If an app is already assigned to a key, you see the app listed. Otherwise, you see the text *No Shortcut.*

4. **Choose a letter to assign an app to that key.**

   For example, choose the A key.

5. **Select an app to assign to the Quick Launch key.**

   From the scrolling menu, pluck an app, such as the Amazon Kindle app.

6. **Repeat Steps 4 and 5 to assign more apps to Quick Launch keys.**

To use a Quick Launch shortcut, press and hold the Search soft button, and then touch the Quick Launch key shortcut, such as Search+A to launch the app associated with the A key.

To reassign an app to a key, repeat the steps in this section and choose a new app in Step 5.

To remove an app from a key, long-press its entry on the Quick Launch screen. Touch the OK button to confirm that you're clearing the key.

Use Sliding-Keyboard Menu Shortcuts

A quick way to access menu commands is to use the sliding keyboard. After pressing the Menu soft key, you can press certain keys on the keyboard to quickly access the commands that are displayed.

For example, pressing the Menu key while using the Browser app displays the onscreen menu. Pressing the B key at this point chooses the Bookmarks command, which is the only command on the menu that begins with the letter *B*. **Note:** This trick doesn't work all the time.

Some menus feature the shortcut keys on the menu itself, as shown in Figure 16-1. In that case, you can access any command by pressing the Menu soft button (to display the menu) and then pressing the corresponding key on the sliding keyboard.

Figure 16-1: Sliding-keyboard menu shortcuts.

For example, in Figure 16-1, the sliding keyboard shortcut for the Downloads command is Menu+D. Press the Menu soft button and then press the D key on the sliding keyboard to display the Downloads window. You don't even have to touch the More command to see the additional menu items; simply press the Menu soft button, and then touch the shortcut key on the sliding keyboard.

  ✔ When no keyboard shortcuts are apparent, you use the sliding keyboard's arrow keys to navigate the menus. Press the OK key to choose a command.

  ✔ You don't have to press the Shift key to use a keyboard shortcut. I use capital letters for readability, which is why you see Menu+B instead of Menu+b, for example.

In-Pocket Detection

I'm a big fan of wearing earphones with my Droid 4. I enjoy talking hands-free, probably because of my Italian background. So I answer the call, insert the earphones, lock the phone, and thrust it into my pocket. With the phone locked, you don't need to worry about the call being accidentally muted or disconnected.

Actually, locking the phone is an extra step. That's because you can have the phone locked automatically whenever it's put into your pocket, thanks to the Droid 4's in-pocket detection feature. Obey these steps to activate it:

1. **At the Home screen, press the Menu soft button.**

2. **Choose Settings and then Display.**

3. **Place a green check mark by the In-Pocket Detection option.**

Now, whenever you thrust your phone into your pocket, it locks automatically.

Contact Quick Actions

You may have noticed that a contact's picture contains three dots below the image. These three dots appear whether the image is a photo or the stock Android icon. They hold significance in that they indicate the availability of the Quick Actions menu for that contact, as shown in Figure 16-2.

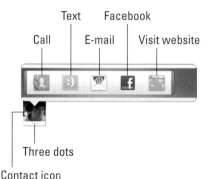

Figure 16-2: Quick Actions for a contact.

Summon the Quick Actions menu by long-pressing the contact's image.

The number and variety of icons on the Quick Actions menu depends on how much information is available for the contact. But no matter where the contact's icon is found, as long as you see those three dots, you can see the Quick Actions menu.

Add Spice to Dictation

I feel that too few people use dictation, despite how handy it can be — especially for text messaging. Anyway, if you've used dictation, you might have noticed that it occasionally censors some of the words you utter. Perhaps you're the kind of person who won't put up with that kind of s***.

Relax. You can lift the vocal censorship ban by following these steps:

1. **At the Home screen, press the Menu soft button.**

2. **Choose Settings, and then choose Voice Input and Output.**

3. **Choose Voice Recognizer Settings.**

4. **Remove the check mark by the option Block Offensive Words.**

And just what are offensive words? I would think that *censorship* is an offensive word. But no; apparently only a few choice words fall into this category. I won't print them here, because the Droid 4 censor retains the initial letter and generally makes the foul language easy to guess. D***.

Add a Word to the Dictionary

Betcha didn't know that the Droid 4 has a dictionary. The dictionary is used to keep track of words you type — words that may not be recognized as being spelled properly.

Words unknown to the Droid 4 appear with a red-dashed underline onscreen. To add one of these words to the dictionary, follow these steps:

1. **Long-press a red-underlined word.**

2. **From the Edit Text menu, choose the command Add *Word* to Dictionary, where *Word* is the word you long-pressed.**

    The command is at the bottom of the menu; scroll down the menu using your finger.

3. **Use the Edit Word dialog box to modify the word, if you need to.**

    For example, remove the *s* if you want to add the root of a plural word.

4. Touch the OK button.

The word is added to the Droid 4 dictionary and is no longer flagged as misspelled.

To review the contents of the dictionary, open the Settings app and choose Language & Keyboard and then User Dictionary. You see a list of words you've added. Touch a word to edit it or to delete it from the dictionary. You can manually add words to the dictionary by pressing the Menu soft button and choosing the Add command.

The Favorites Widget

The Favorites widget is preinstalled on the main Home screen, right up top. It lists up to 20 of your favorite contacts, though only the top four are visible on the widget. To see the full boatload, swipe down on the widget. To hide the full load, swipe the widget back up again.

Choosing a contact from the Favorites widget displays the contact's Quick Actions menu, shown in Figure 16-2. Touch the Phone icon to dial the contact, the Text icon to text, and so on.

- ✔ If the Favorites widget isn't affixed to your phone's Home screen, you can easily add it: See Chapter 15 for directions on adding widgets. The Favorites widget is officially named Favorite Contacts.

- ✔ Favorite contacts are set in the Contacts app. See Chapter 5.

- ✔ You can rearrange the contacts in the Favorites widget: Long-press a contact's image and then drag it to another location. The remaining icons reshuffle their position.

Smart Actions

The Droid 4 features an automation tool called Smart Actions. Like other automation tools, or task-scheduling utilities, the Smart Actions tool lets you identify various triggers and set actions for when those triggers occur. The whole idea is to automate certain repetitive tasks.

For example, when I visit the local library, the phone should be silenced. Sometimes I forget, which is embarrassing. With Smart Actions, however, I can create a rule where the phone automatically recognizes my location and automatically silences itself. The rule is shown in Figure 16-3.

Figure 16-3: The Quiet in the Library rule.

To create that rule, or similar rules, follow these general steps:

1. **Start the Smart Actions app.**

   It's found on the Apps menu.

2. **Touch the green plus (+) icon to create a new rule.**

3. **Choose Start from Scratch.**

   The other options, especially Add a Sample, are good for when you're starting out because they give you an idea of the app's usefulness and potential.

4. **Touch the plus button next to Triggers to add an event.**

   Numerous trigger events are available. I used the Location trigger for my Library rule. I then added the Library as a location by searching for it on the map.

   A useful trigger is Timeframe. You can use that trigger to silence the phone overnight or simply change the ringtone.

5. **Touch the plus button next to Actions to direct the phone to do something once the trigger event happens.**

   You can choose from plenty of actions, ranging from opening apps to changing phone settings.

6. **Add more actions, if required.**

   You're not limited to only one action. For example, you could silence the phone, lower the brightness, and even send a text message to let your spouse know that you're taking a nap.

7. **Name the Smart Action.**

   Type its name in the New Rule text box.

8. **Touch the Add Rule button.**

   The rule is created.

 The Smart Actions app alerts you with suggestions from time to time. You'll see a Smart Actions notification appear, similar to what's shown in the margin. Choose that notification to see what the phone suggests. Oftentimes the suggestions are worthy and, unlike dreaming up a rule from scratch, are easy to create.

Find Your Lost Cell Phone

Someday, you may lose your Droid 4 — for a few panic-filled seconds or forever. The hardware solution is to weld to the phone a heavy object, such as a bowling ball or a steam shovel, yet that kind of defeats the entire mobile/wireless paradigm. The software solution is to use a cell phone locator service.

Cell phone locator services employ apps that use a phone's cellular signal as well as its GPS to help locate the missing gizmo. These types of apps are available at the Play Store (see Chapter 12). I've not tried them all, and many of them require a subscription service or registration at a website to complete the process.

Here are some suggestions for cell phone locator apps:

- Wheres My Droid
- Lookout Mobile Security
- Mobile Phone Locator

The Task Manager

 If you want to get your hands dirty with some behind-the-scenes stuff on your phone, Task Manager is the app for you. It's not for everyone, so feel free to skip this section if you want to use your phone without acquiring any computer nerd sickness that you have otherwise successfully avoided.

The Task Manager app is found on the Apps menu. Its main interface is shown in Figure 16-4. All the phone's currently running apps are displayed, along with trivial information about each one: The CPU item shows how much processor power the app is consuming, and the RAM item shows how much storage the app occupies.

Selected apps   Running apps

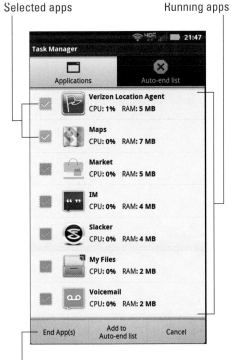

Menu shows up only when items are selected

Figure 16-4: Managing your tasks.

You can use Task Manager to kill off tasks that are hogging too much CPU time or memory or that just bug the stuffing from your couch. Touch items you want to kill, and then touch the End App(s) button. The apps are silently snuffed out.

A nifty feature in Task Manager is the Auto-End list. When apps have been assigned to this list, they automatically exit two minutes after the display times out. To add apps to the list, select them from the main screen (refer to Figure 16-4) and touch the Add to Auto-End List button at the bottom of the screen.

 ✔ There's no need to kill off an app flagged as "not running."

 ✔ Task Manager doesn't delete apps; it merely stops them from running. To delete an app, use the Play Store, as discussed in Chapter 12.

 ✔ Also see Chapter 12 on using the Force Stop button to kill an app run amok.

 ✔ The Android operating system does an excellent job of managing apps. If resources are needed for another app, Android automatically closes any open apps as needed. Futzing with Task Manager is unnecessary, unless you just enjoy messing with such a thing.

Chapter 17

Ten Favorite Apps

*N*othing stirs up controversy like stating that 10 Android apps are more worthy than the 500,000-plus apps available at the Play Store. Even so, when I started out with the Droid Zero twenty years ago, I wanted to see a list of worthy apps, or even apps recommended by friends. Lamentably, that was a long time before anyone else had a Droid phone of any type, so I was forced to wait. Thanks to the suggestions in this chapter, you won't have to wait to get started with some apps on your Droid 4.

AK Notepad

 For some odd reason, your Droid 4 doesn't come with a note-taking app. Anyway, a good choice for an app to fill that void is AK Notepad. You can type or dictate short messages and memos, which I find handy.

For example, before a recent visit to the hardware store, I dictated a list of items I needed by using AK Notepad. I also keep some important items as notes — things that I often forget or don't care to remember, such as frequent flyer numbers and my dress shirt and suit size (like I ever need that info).

CardStar

 The handy CardStar app answers the question, "Why do I have all these store rewards cards?" They're not credit cards — they're marketing cards designed for customer loyalty programs. Rather than tote those cards around in your wallet or on your keychain, you can scan a card's bar code using your phone and save the "card" on the phone.

After you store your loyalty cards in the phone, you simply run the CardStar app to summon the appropriate merchant. Show the checkout person your phone or scan the bar code yourself. CardStar makes it easy.

Dolphin Browser

 Although I don't mind using the Browser app that comes with my phone, it's despised by many Android users. A better and more popular alternative is Dolphin Browser.

Like many popular computer browsers, Dolphin Browser features a tabbed interface, which works much better than the silly multiple-window interface of the standard Browser app.

Gesture Search

 The Gesture Search app provides a new way to find information on your phone. Rather than use a keyboard or dictate, you simply draw on the touchscreen the first letter of whatever you're searching for.

Start the Google Search app to begin a search. Use your finger to draw a big letter on the screen. After you draw a letter, search results appear on the screen. You can continue drawing more letters to refine the search or touch a search result.

Gesture Search can find contacts, music, apps, and bookmarks in the Browser app.

Google Finance

 The Google Finance app is an excellent market-tracking tool for folks who are obsessed with the stock market or want to keep an eye on their portfolios. The app offers you an overview of the market and updates to your stocks, as well as links to financial news.

To get the most from this app, configure Google Finance on the web, using your computer. You can create lists of stocks to watch, which are then instantly synchronized with your Droid 4. You can visit Google Finance on the web at www.google.com/finance.

As with other Google services, Google Finance is provided to you for free, as part of your Google account.

Google Sky Map

 Ever look up into the sky and say, "What the heck is that?" Unless it's a bird, an airplane, a satellite, a UFO, or a superhero, Google Sky Map helps you find what it is. You may learn that a particularly bright star in the sky is, in fact, the planet Jupiter.

The Google Sky Map app is elegant. It basically turns your Droid 4 into a window you can look through to identify objects in the night sky. Just start the app and hold the phone up to the sky. Pan the phone to identify planets, stars, and constellations.

 Google Sky Map promotes using the phone without touching its screen. For this reason, the screen goes blank after a spell, which is merely the phone's power-saving mode. If you plan extensive stargazing with Google Sky Map, consider resetting the screen time-out. Refer to Chapter 15 for details.

Movies

 The Movies app is your phone's gateway to Hollywood. It lists currently running films and films that are opening, and it has links to your local theaters with showtimes and other information. The app is also tied into the popular Rotten Tomatoes website for reviews and feedback. If you enjoy going to the movies, you'll find the Movies app a valuable addition to your Droid 4's app inventory.

QuickPic

 Face it: The My Gallery app isn't the best or most logical way to view and organize pictures on your phone. The app is also not the easiest thing to figure out; I know I've been frustrated by it endlessly. A better solution is the free app QuickPic. It's fast. It makes sense. I recommend checking it out.

SportsTap

 I admit to not being a sports nut, so it's difficult for me to identify with the craving to have the latest scores, news, and schedules. The sports nuts in my life, however, tell me that the very best app for that purpose is a handy thing named SportsTap.

Rather than blather on about something I'm not into, I'll just ask that you take my advice and obtain SportsTap. I believe you'll be thrilled.

Voice Recorder

 Your Droid 4 has the hardware necessary to record your voice or other sounds. An app that can accomplish that task is Voice Recorder. It has an elegant and simple interface: Touch the big Record button to start recording. Make a note for yourself or record a friend doing his Daffy Duck impression.

Previous recordings are stored in a list on the Voice Recorder main screen. Every recording is shown with its title, the date and time of the recording, and the recording duration.

Avoiding Android viruses

How can you tell which apps are legitimate and which might be viruses or evil apps that do odd things to your Droid 4? Well, you can't. In fact, most people can't, because most evil apps don't advertise themselves as such.

The key to knowing whether an app is evil is to look at what it does, as described in Chapter 12. If a simple grocery-list app uses the phone's text-messaging service and the app doesn't need to send text messages, it's suspect.

In the history of the Android operating system, only a handful of malicious apps have been distributed, and most of them were found on phones used in Asia. Google routinely removes malicious apps from the Google Play Store, and a feature of the Android operating system even lets Google remotely wipe such apps from your phone, so you're pretty safe.

Generally speaking, avoid "hacker" apps, porn, and apps that use social engineering to make you do things on your phone that you wouldn't otherwise do, such as text an overseas number to see racy pictures of politicians or celebrities.

Index

• Z •

Apple & Macs

iPad For Dummies
978-0-470-58027-1

iPhone For Dummies,
4th Edition
978-0-470-87870-5

MacBook For
Dummies, 3rd Edition
978-0-470-76918-8

Mac OS X Snow
Leopard For
Dummies
978-0-470-43543-4

Business

Bookkeeping For
Dummies
978-0-7645-9848-7

Job Interviews
For Dummies,
3rd Edition
978-0-470-17748-8

Resumes For
Dummies,
5th Edition
978-0-470-08037-5

Starting an
Online Business
For Dummies,
6th Edition
978-0-470-60210-2

Stock Investing
For Dummies,
3rd Edition
978-0-470-40114-9

Successful
Time Management
For Dummies
978-0-470-29034-7

Computer Hardware

BlackBerry
For Dummies,
4th Edition
978-0-470-60700-8

Computers For
Seniors
For Dummies,
2nd Edition
978-0-470-53483-0

PCs For Dummies,
Windows 7 Edition
978-0-470-46542-4

Laptops For
Dummies,
4th Edition
978-0-470-57829-2

Cooking & Entertaining

Cooking Basics
For Dummies,
3rd Edition
978-0-7645-7206-7

Wine For Dummies,
4th Edition
978-0-470-04579-4

Diet & Nutrition

Dieting For Dummies,
2nd Edition
978-0-7645-4149-0

Nutrition For
Dummies,
4th Edition
978-0-471-79868-2

Weight Training
For Dummies,
3rd Edition
978-0-471-76845-6

Digital Photography

Digital SLR Cameras
& Photography For
Dummies, 3rd Edition
978-0-470-46606-3

Photoshop Elements 8
For Dummies
978-0-470-52967-6

Gardening

Gardening Basics
For Dummies
978-0-470-03749-2

Organic Gardening
For Dummies,
2nd Edition
978-0-470-43067-5

Green/Sustainable

Raising Chickens
For Dummies
978-0-470-46544-8

Green Cleaning
For Dummies
978-0-470-39106-8

Health

Diabetes For
Dummies,
3rd Edition
978-0-470-27086-8

Food Allergies
For Dummies
978-0-470-09584-3

Living Gluten-Free
For Dummies,
2nd Edition
978-0-470-58589-4

Hobbies/General

Chess For Dummies,
2nd Edition
978-0-7645-8404-6

Drawing
Cartoons & Comics
For Dummies
978-0-470-42683-8

Knitting For Dummies,
2nd Edition
978-0-470-28747-7

Organizing
For Dummies
978-0-7645-5300-4

Su Doku For
Dummies
978-0-470-01892-7

Home Improvement

Home Maintenance
For Dummies,
2nd Edition
978-0-470-43063-7

Home Theater
For Dummies,
3rd Edition
978-0-470-41189-6

Living the
Country Lifestyle
All-in-One
For Dummies
978-0-470-43061-3

Solar Power Your
Home
For Dummies,
2nd Edition
978-0-470-59678-4

Available wherever books are sold. For more information or to order direct: U.S. customers visit
www.dummies.com or call 1-877-762-2974. U.K. customers visit www.wileyeurope.com or call (0)
1243 843291. Canadian customers visit www.wiley.ca or call 1-800-567-4797.

Internet

Blogging For
Dummies,
3rd Edition
978-0-470-61996-4

eBay For Dummies,
6th Edition
978-0-470-49741-8

Facebook For
Dummies, 3rd Edition
978-0-470-87804-0

Web Marketing
For Dummies,
2nd Edition
978-0-470-37181-7

WordPress
For Dummies,
3rd Edition
978-0-470-59274-8

Language & Foreign Language

French For Dummies
978-0-7645-5193-2

Italian Phrases
For Dummies
978-0-7645-7203-6

Spanish For
Dummies, 2nd Edition
978-0-470-87855-2

Spanish For
Dummies, Audio Set
978-0-470-09585-0

Math & Science

Algebra I
For Dummies,
2nd Edition
978-0-470-55964-2

Biology
For Dummies,
2nd Edition
978-0-470-59875-7

Calculus For
Dummies
978-0-7645-2498-1

Chemistry For
Dummies
978-0-7645-5430-8

Microsoft Office

Excel 2010 For
Dummies
978-0-470-48953-6

Office 2010 All-in-One
For Dummies
978-0-470-49748-7

Office 2010 For
Dummies,
Book + DVD Bundle
978-0-470-62698-6

Word 2010 For
Dummies
978-0-470-48772-3

Music

Guitar For Dummies,
2nd Edition
978-0-7645-9904-0

iPod & iTunes
For Dummies,
8th Edition
978-0-470-87871-2

Piano Exercises
For Dummies
978-0-470-38765-8

Parenting & Education

Parenting For
Dummies,
2nd Edition
978-0-7645-5418-6

Type 1 Diabetes
For Dummies
978-0-470-17811-9

Pets

Cats For Dummies,
2nd Edition
978-0-7645-5275-5

Dog Training
For Dummies,
3rd Edition
978-0-470-60029-0

Puppies For
Dummies,
2nd Edition
978-0-470-03717-1

Religion & Inspiration

The Bible For
Dummies
978-0-7645-5296-0

Catholicism For
Dummies
978-0-7645-5391-2

Women in the Bible
For Dummies
978-0-7645-8475-6

Self-Help & Relationship

Anger Management
For Dummies
978-0-470-03715-7

Overcoming Anxiety
For Dummies,
2nd Edition
978-0-470-57441-6

Sports

Baseball
For Dummies,
3rd Edition
978-0-7645-7537-2

Basketball
For Dummies,
2nd Edition
978-0-7645-5248-9

Golf For Dummies,
3rd Edition
978-0-471-76871-5

Web Development

Web Design
All-in-One
For Dummies
978-0-470-41796-6

Web Sites
Do-It-Yourself
For Dummies,
2nd Edition
978-0-470-56520-9

Windows 7

Windows 7
For Dummies
978-0-470-49743-2

Windows 7
For Dummies,
Book + DVD Bundle
978-0-470-52398-8

Windows 7 All-in-One
For Dummies
978-0-470-48763-1

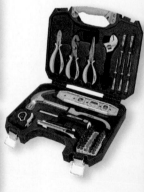